The Listener's Guides
Edited by Alan Rich

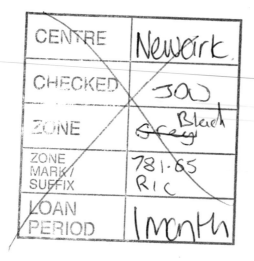

JAZZ
Morley Jones

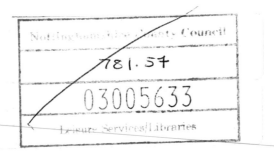

BLANDFORD PRESS

POOLE   DORSET

A QUARTO BOOK

First published in the U.K. 1980
by Blandford Press Ltd.
Link House, West Street,
Poole, Dorset, BH15 1LL

The *Listener's Guide* series was conceived and
edited by John Smallwood
Design: Joan Peckolick
Design assistant: Elizabeth Fox
Editorial assistant: Gene Santoro
Production: Millie Falcaro
Picture Research: Michelle Flaum

Produced and prepared by Quarto Marketing, Ltd.

Manufactured in the United States of America
Printed and bound by The Maple-Vail Manufacturing Group

British Library Cataloguing in Publication Data
Rich, Alan
The listener's guide to jazz.—
(The listener's guides).
1.   Jazz music
I.   Title
785.4'2'0904   ML3506

CONTENTS

AUTHOR'S NOTE

The history of jazz doesn't lend itself to precise categories. The music is too new, and its chronology is too easily muddled: some of the most daring members of its avant-garde have been dead for ten years or more, while some representatives of its earliest era play on. Many of its most important figures have contributed mightily to more than one jazz style or period.

Nonetheless, styles and periods do exist in jazz, and most jazz musicians of note owe primary allegiance to one or the other of them. In the following pages, thirty-eight individuals (and two ensembles) are singled out for special notice. In ten chapters, which are mostly devoted to styles and periods, each musician or group has been placed in the most appropriate context.

Sometimes, this was easy: Louis Armstrong was a New Orleans musician, no matter when and where he played. Sometimes, it was more difficult—as in the case of Sidney Bechet, another New Orleans musician. Bechet was less clearly tied to his origins in his later career than Armstrong was, but he nevertheless has ended up in the New Orleans chapter. Two figures—Duke Ellington and Miles Davis—seem so protean, so influential, and so fiercely original as to demand a chapter of their own.

Some of the artists included here are generally considered to be among the giants of jazz—among them, Louis Armstrong, James P. Johnson, Coleman Hawkins, Charlie Parker, Billie Holiday, and John Coltrane. On the other hand, there are people who will question my saving places in my pantheon for musicians like Bennie Moten, Lennie Tristano, Eddie Jefferson, or John Surman. The only proper answer is that any history must include not only the indisputable greats, but also those who have originated or typified a stylistic dialect or innovation of more than passing interest.

Some final notes: musicians are listed under the form of their names by which they are best known and their full or given names are given in parentheses. Nicknames that are not commonly used in referring to these musicians, colorful though they may be ("Little Jazz" for Roy Eldridge, "Newk" for Sonny Rollins, and so on), are not mentioned. Each musician is identified only by those instruments that he or she most usually plays. The recordings listed for each artist were chosen as representative examples of his or her best work. The original LP release is listed under the selected recordings except where well-annotated reissues exist. In many cases, albums have been re-released in several forms over the years, and Japanese and European pressings are also available of some of them. With the current chaos in the record industry, the extensive corporate changes and realignments, the task of keeping abreast of labels and numbers would drive anyone to reserve a spot at St. James Infirmary.

—M.J.

1

INTRODUCTION

Two unpleasant tasks immediately confront any writer who undertakes to fashion a survey of jazz: the first (and more vexing) is defining the word *jazz;* the second is describing the dispersion of jazz from its putative birthplace, New Orleans, into the urban North and Midwest, and thus into the mainstream of American musical life. The latter task will be addressed in Chapter Two of this volume. The former will be tackled here.

The problem with defining jazz is not that it eludes definition, but that definition seems somehow beside the point. Jazz has not been with us for very long, after all: Jelly Roll Morton somewhat extravagantly claimed that he had "invented" jazz in 1902. Morton aside, most scholars of the subject agree that it dates, as a recognizable musical idiom, from the first few years of the century. Throughout this rather brief history, jazz has been written and played largely intuitively, without excessive regard for its (largely accidental) formal characteristics. This is not to say that it is an unstructured musical form or that, however common and informal its origins may have been, it is a naïve one. The codification of its formal aspects has just never been very important to those who have created it.

Some Definitions of Jazz

There is some disagreement about whether or not jazz is a kind of folk music, but it is certainly something typically American—spontaneous, accessible, and animated by a spirit of adventure. Furthermore, jazz is traditional, in the sense that it has accepted usages, stylistic trappings, and jargon, both literal and musical, that are transmitted within and between cultures by non-verbal means.

Instrumental technique and theories of composition and improvisation can be taught in the classroom, but the feeling for jazz is either there or it isn't. Louis Armstrong's remark to the effect that people who have to ask what jazz is "are never going to know" has often been quoted. Of course, there are orthodox definitions of jazz. For instance, Webster's Third New International Dictionary identifies it as "American music developed from religious and secular songs ... and other popular music and characterized by improvisation, syncopated rhythms, contrapuntal ensemble playing, special melodic features (as flatted notes, blues notes) peculiar to the individual player, and the introduction of vocal techniques (as portamento) into instrumental performances." In other words, jazz musicians make it up as they go along, accentuate the offbeat in a rhythmic figure, play one melody while somebody else is playing another one, and slide all over their instruments.

Other definitions mention rubato (disregard for the strict time values of the notes); polyrhythms (contrasting rhythms played simultaneously); unique tonal colorations (including such essentially non-musical effects as "growling" or "laughing" sounds played by horns); glissando (the rapid sliding of the finger along a string or a keyboard); and the frequent use of such devices as riffs (single phrases repeated over and over) and breaks (brief improvised interludes, usually four bars in duration, between phrases). To these, the famous black poet Langston Hughes added what he considered to be one of the basic elements of jazz, the "joy of playing"—which he defined in part as a "happy, dancing quality, that brings musicians . . . together. . . ." There is no question that jazz most often has an emotional impact on listener and musician alike.

Most of the elements mentioned in classic definitions are indeed present in much of jazz, but any one or more of them can be missing in music that is still good, valid jazz. A particularly good further analysis of the constituent elements of jazz, including examples in musical notation, appears in *The New Edition of the Encyclopedia of Jazz,* by jazz critic Leonard Feather, in a section entitled "The Anatomy of Jazz." However, Feather warns the reader "constant listening" will be necessary in order to understand distinctions noted in the text. Even half an hour with the records of artists like Louis Armstrong, Duke Ellington, Charlie Parker, or the Art Ensemble of Chicago will tell the listener more about jazz than written words ever could.

Jazz on Record

The recording process developed approximately contemporaneously with jazz. The first cylinder recordings were made by Thomas Edison (and independently by the French scientist Charles Gros) in 1877, but recordings of music in commercial quantities did not become widely available until the 1890s. Even so, it wasn't until the emergence of Victor and Columbia as major record labels in 1902 that recorded music came within the reach of the general populace. This process has been inestimably important to the growth and refinement of music, and especially jazz. An improvised musical form must be recorded in order to be preserved: it must be heard over and over if it is to influence performers and make sense to its audiences.

The phonograph record has been much more than a, er, record of jazz: it has also been the reason that much of it has been played. Recording studios have given musicians a venue they could not often find in concert halls or popular arenas. Geographically and philosophically disparate musicians have been brought together on the same disk; whole careers have been built on vinyl.

Of course, other careers have slipped between the grooves. Pioneer New Orleans cornetist Buddy Bolden apparently never recorded; bandleader Jean Goldkette, whose bands included such major jazz figures as Bix Beiderbecke, Frank Trumbauer, Joe Venuti, and Eddie Lang, was rarely permitted by his record company to record jazz. Throughout the history of jazz, scores of first-rate "regional" musicians (mostly from regions other than New York or Los Angeles) have been either under- or unrecorded.

Records, then, give us a somewhat incomplete picture of jazz, but the picture they do give is vivid and exciting, the only lasting, retrievable picture that we have.

–1–

No one city can claim jazz as its own: jazz didn't have a literal birthplace any more than any other endeavor or art form did. Pioneer jazz musicians, some of whom are still alive, have recalled the early existence of black street bands and ragtime orchestras throughout the Midwest and Southwest; pianist Eubie Blake, born in Baltimore in 1883, remembers playing ragtime there as a teenager (his approximate contemporary, bassist Pops Foster, has noted, "What's called jazz today was called ragtime back then"); and pioneer jazz trumpeter Jabbo Smith, among others, has indicated that Charleston, South Carolina, had its own thriving jazz scene early in the century.

However, New Orleans was the most important incubator of jazz and produced its first two really famous offspring—Louis Armstrong and King Oliver. All the many elements that seem to have contributed to the creation of jazz were most evident there. It was a wealthy, cosmopolitan, racially diverse, relatively unbigoted city, a busy port that received the goods and cultural influences of many nations. It was a place whose virtues included a temperate climate that encouraged street life and a penchant for the pursuit of pleasure, outdoors and in, that cut across lines of class and color. It was the perfect environment for the nourishment of jazz. If jazz, or something very like jazz, existed simultaneously, or even previously, in other areas, it was in New Orleans that it grew strong and popular and the complex grafting of this hybrid art took place.

Jazz was nothing if not a hybrid. Among its original forebears were West African music and Caribbean music (particularly the quite different styles of Haiti and Cuba). However, it is widely agreed today that the African and Caribbean "primitive" origins of jazz have often been unfairly overemphasized, and that European and North American influences were much more important than they appear at first to be. Spanish and French popular and classical music certainly influenced the course that jazz took. New Orleans was French for the first forty-six years of its existence and Spanish for the next thirty-six; opera and concert music had been popular there since before the Civil War, and formal musical training was hardly a rarity, for either whites or blacks. Traditional music from the British Isles played its part—both directly, through the secular music of immigrants to North America, and indirectly, through liturgical music—and the music of both the white Cajuns (French-Canadian immigrants to Louisiana) and the black "Creoles of color" were significant in the development of jazz.

The more immediate ancestors of jazz include: black folk music like work songs, spirituals, plantation reels and jumps, and blues; ragtime—both in its formal sense, as typified by the piano compositions of Scott Joplin, and in its looser, street band incarnation; and, perhaps most of all, the brass band music, some of it leaning toward ragtime, that was so much a part of the "pleasure clubs" and the fraternal organizations in New Orleans and elsewhere around the turn of the century.

The first black New Orleans musician to be captured on wax was trombonist Kid Ory—in 1921, and in Los Angeles; but the

5

skill and stylistic certainty with which early New Orleans jazz musicians played when they finally were recorded indicates that there was a good deal of dedicated music-making going on in their city in those days.

It was in this early, unrecorded New Orleans era that the basic instrumentation of the small jazz band was developed—an instrumentation that has been used, with variations, in virtually every period of jazz since that time. The formula was simple: to provide the fundamental environment, there were three rhythm instruments (string bass, sometimes replaced in the early days by tuba; guitar, banjo, or, when circumstances permitted, piano; and, of course, drums). To this would be added one or two brass instruments to play the melody or melody and harmony (cornet or cornets—later replaced by the cornet's close relative, the trumpet—or cornet/trumpet and trombone). Finally, there would be one or two reed instruments for further textural complexity (almost always clarinet until the saxophone was introduced to jazz in the 1920s).

This was also the period in which the first great soloists of jazz were developing their characteristic styles. Among these artists were cornetists Louis Armstrong, King Oliver, Freddie Keppard, and Bunk Johnson; clarinetists Johnny Dodds, Jimmy Noone, and Sidney Bechet (who soon adopted the soprano saxophone); trombonist Kid Ory; and pianist Jelly Roll Morton.

The music these men played was something quite different from what had been played by their immediate precursors. It was freer, more casual, "hotter," but at the same time blended into a smooth, consistent unit. It was a new kind of music, and although it had not yet been named as such, it was jazz.

KING OLIVER *(Joseph Oliver) (1885–1938)*

King Oliver was born somewhere in Louisiana, probably on a plantation where his mother worked, and was raised in New Orleans. As a teenager, he studied trombone for a time before settling with cornet. In his teens and early twenties, Oliver played with popular pre-jazz bands like the Melrose, the Olympia, the Magnolia, the Eagle, and the Original Superior. He joined Kid Ory's band briefly around 1913 or 1914 and led his own first bands at that time. In 1917, he rejoined Ory, who by now thought enough of the young man's playing to dub him "King."

Oliver traveled north with the Bill Johnson band and with the Lawrence Duhé band, which he later took over. In New Orleans, Oliver had been a great influence on Louis Armstrong, among others. Armstrong had filled his chair in the Ory band, and, in 1922, Oliver brought him to Chicago to play second cornet in what "King" had dubbed the Creole Jazz Band. Other members of the group included Johnny Dodds and his brother, drummer Baby Dodds; trombonist Honoré Dutrey; and pianist and vocalist Lil Hardin (who later became Mrs. Armstrong). Later, Kid Ory himself joined the group, along with Jimmie Noone and clarinetists Barney Bigard and Albert Nicholas. It was strong, intense music, with integrated ensemble passages and disciplined but frequently exciting collective improvisation.

Armstrong left Oliver in 1924, and later that year the group disbanded. Oliver played with other orchestras for about two years, then formed a larger band, the Dixie Syncopators. With them he recorded one of his own compositions, "Sugar Foot Stomp," a new version of "Dippermouth Blues" (which he had recorded with the Creole Jazz Band). On the new record, he played a lean, elegantly shaded solo that became a milestone of jazz improvisation.

In 1928, Oliver's pianist, Luis Russell, left to form a band of his own, taking many of the Syncopators with him. In the late 1920s and early 1930s, Oliver worked off and on, sometimes without a band of his own and sometimes forming bands that didn't last for very long. The Depression had seriously affected the cabaret business, jobs were few, and Oliver's health was bad. In 1936, he settled in Savannah, where he ran a fruit stall and worked in a pool hall. He died there of a cerebral hemorrhage, forgotten temporarily by many of his fellow musicians.

Even if he had done no more than provide the inspiration and the technical model for Louis Armstrong, Oliver would have been an important jazz figure. As it was, he was also a well-disciplined sophisticated musician who showed that jazz could retain its spontaneity and emotional power even when played with control. His Creole Jazz Band probably did more than any other early jazz group to show people just what the music was all about.

Selected Recordings

King Oliver's Jazz Band, 1923 (Smithsonian)
Back o' Town (Riverside)
King Oliver and His Dixie Syncopaters (two volumes, VJM)
King Oliver in New York (RCA)

The recordings on the Smithsonian collection are from the middle period of Oliver's long, early-1920s engagement in Chicago and include Louis Armstrong. The VJM recordings feature Oliver's larger band, formed in 1924, and include his famous cornet solo on "Sugar Foot Stomp." The RCA tracks are late recordings, made when Oliver was in decline, including standards like "Frankie and Johnny," "St. James Infirmary," and the ironically titled "Too Late."

LOUIS ARMSTRONG *(1900–71)*

Louis Armstrong was born into poverty and brought up in a tough neighborhood of New Orleans. Although as a child he had sung for money on the streets with his cohorts, he had never played an instrument until he was arrested, at the age of 13 or 14 (for firing a gun into the air) and remanded to the Colored Waifs' Home. There, he was given music lessons and was inducted into the Home's band, first on drums, briefly on trombone, and finally on cornet.

When he was released from the Home, he gave up music temporarily to work at a variety of jobs, but soon he formed a small band with drummer Joe Lindsey, and eventually he was befriended by King Oliver. He replaced Oliver in Kid Ory's band, then played with pianist Fate Marable on riverboats between New Orleans and St. Louis.

Armstrong joined King Oliver's band in Chicago in 1922, married Oliver's pianist, Lil Hardin, and, in mid-1924, left the group. He joined Fletcher Henderson's band in New York, where his fame grew fast, and then played for a time with his wife's band in Chicago. He switched to trumpet and in 1926, working with violinist/bandleader Carroll Dickerson, he was billed as "World's Greatest Trumpet Player." Throughout the latter 1920s, he played with other bands and led his own band, which included pianist Earl Hines. Simultaneously, he made a series of records with pick-up groups, under the name "Louis Armstrong's Hot Five" or "Hot Seven," that was to affect the course of jazz profoundly.

The "Hot" groups, which included musicians like Johnny and Baby Dodds, Kid Ory, Zutty Singleton, Lil Hardin, and Earl Hines, were everything that King Oliver's Creole Jazz Band had been, and more—disciplined but exciting, intelligent but visceral, serious but fun. Armstrong's playing was technically superb by this time, and he had taken Oliver's elegant style and further refined it. His playing was deceptively simple, almost cautious, though rarely without fire. Most of his fellow musicians were at the peak of their powers. Some sixty "Hot" records were released over a three-year period. Together, they are one of the most impressive bodies of work in the jazz canon, and they gave jazz its first superstar. By 1929, largely because of Armstrong, jazz had taken hold in the United States and had gained a following in Europe. It had become a recognizable, appreciated musical form, as familiar to white audiences as it was to black ones.

In 1929, Armstrong moved from Chicago to New York, and

from being a top-notch New Orleans jazzman to being an international star. He toured as featured soloist with a number of bands, sometimes working almost every night of the year. In 1932, he went to Europe for the first time. In 1936, he made what was to be the first of many films, *Pennies from Heaven,* with Bing Crosby. In the late 1930s and early 1940s, Armstrong was the star of Luis Russell's big band, and in 1944 and 1945, he led his own band again. In 1947, he formed a small group, Louis Armstrong and His Jazz All-Stars, which included clarinetist Barney Bigard, trombonist Jack Teagarden, and drummer "Big Sid" Catlett. For most of the rest of his life, Armstrong fronted an "All-Star" small band. Later members of the group included such genuine stars as Earl Hines, clarinetists Edmond Hall and Barney Bigard, cornetist Bobby Hackett, trombonist/vocalist Trummy Young, and drummer Cozy Cole.

During his lifetime, Armstrong recorded with vocalists like Billie Holiday, Bing Crosby, Ella Fitzgerald, and the Danish folk duo Nina and Frederick and with orchestras led by such notables as Sy Oliver, Benny Carter, Gordon Jenkins, and Russ Garcia. He made small band recordings with Oscar Peterson and Duke Ellington and several with the Dukes of Dixieland, a Dixieland revival group that was popular in the late 1950s and early 1960s. Armstrong continued to appear in films, among them, *The Glenn Miller Story, High Society, The Five Pennies,* and *Paris Blues.* His recording of the title song from his last film, *Hello Dolly,* made him something of a star to a whole new generation of listeners.

There has sometimes been a mistaken tendency to downplay Armstrong's importance as a vocalist. Although he undeniably sang many mediocre pop songs in his long career (and played them, too), his rough, warm, open vocal quality and his popularization of wordless "scat" singing influenced the fledgling art of jazz singing tremendously.

Armstrong was a brilliant musician and the first great ground- breaker of jazz. His influence has been incalculable.

Selected Recordings

Louis Armstrong with Fletcher Henderson (BYG)
The Louis Armstrong Story (four volumes, Columbia)
Town Hall Concert (RCA)
Satchmo: A Musical Autobiography of Louis Armstrong (four volumes, Decca)
Ella & Louis (two-record set, Verve)
Porgy and Bess (two-record set , Verve)
Snake Rag (Chiaroscuro)

The album with Fletcher Henderson, on the French BYG label, is a good selection of tracks from Armstrong's stint with the Henderson band in New York. The four-volume Columbia set is essential to any collection. It contains all the landmark Hot Five and Hot Seven recordings, additional work with Earl

Hines, and other recordings of note. The Town Hall album features a particularly good version of the All-Stars, including performances by Jack Teagarden and Bobby Hackett.

The Decca LPs are a fascinating set, recorded throughout the 1950s with various editions of the All-Stars, in which Armstrong narrates and musically illustrates his own rich creative past. *Ella & Louis* is a two-record set of Armstrong and Ella Fitzgerald singing a long program of standards ("Cheek to Cheek," "I'm Putting All My Eggs in One Basket," "Let's Call the Whole Thing Off") with a quartet led by pianist Oscar Peterson. The second Verve album is a classic jazz version of the famous Gershwin opera, with Armstrong both singing and playing in top form. The final LP features a later version of the All-Stars, with Peanuts Hucko and Trummy Young.

JOHNNY DODDS *(1892–1940)*

Clarinetist Johnny Dodds, brother of the seminal New Orleans drummer Baby Dodds, was the leading exponent of the New Orleans clarinet style (particularly after Sidney Bechet started concentrating on soprano saxophone)—warm, reedy, light, and almost offhand.

Like his colleague Louis Armstrong, Dodds played with Kid Ory and Fate Marable and later joined King Oliver in Chicago. He settled into Chicago, organized his own bands, and played with Freddie Keppard and Honoré Dutrey. He recorded with Ory, Oliver, and Jelly Roll Morton. Most importantly, he collaborated with Louis Armstrong on his Hot Five and Hot Seven recordings, where he was a good foil, both strong and languid, for the leader.

Throughout the 1930s, Dodds (with his brother) played minor clubs in Chicago and intermittently drove cabs for a living. He performed almost until he died in 1940.

Selected Recordings

Johnny Dodds and Kid Ory (Epic)
Johnny Dodds Washboard Band (RCA)
The Louis Armstrong Story by Louis Armstrong (four volumes, Columbia)

The Epic LP, from 1926, features Dodds with two related ensembles, the New Orleans Wanderers and the New Orleans Bootblacks; other players include cornetist George Mitchell,

banjoist/guitarist Johnny St. Cyr, pianist Lil (Hardin) Armstrong, and, something of a rarity in those days, an alto saxophonist—Jimmy Walker. The RCA tracks, from 1928, include two illustrious New Orleans pioneers, Natty Dominique on trumpet and Honoré Dutrey on trombone, and feature Baby Dodds on washboard. Some of Dodds' finest playing appears on the Louis Armstrong "Hot" sides, which may be found on the first two volumes of the Columbia set.

SIDNEY BECHET   *(1897–1959)*

Reportedly, Sidney Bechet first picked up a clarinet when he was 6 and, while still a child, he was allowed to sit in with Freddie Keppard. He was self-taught, originally, but later studied with prototypical New Orleans clarinetists George Baquet and Lorenzo Tio, Jr. He played in street bands and with touring carnival orchestras throughout the South and Southwest. Bechet worked briefly with Bunk Johnson, Freddie Keppard, and King Oliver and in 1919, he joined the Southern Syncopated Orchestra of Will Marion Cook, who wrote the first black musical to appear on Broadway, *Clorindy, Or The Origin of the Cakewalk.* This group was not a jazz band, but a concert band with a wide repertoire that included jazz-flavored pieces. While Bechet was on a European tour with the group, the Swiss conductor Ernest Ansermet heard him and described him as "an extraordinary clarinet virtuoso" and an "artist of genius"—an indication not only of Bechet's talent but of the increasingly broad appeal of the newer American music.

Bechet remained in Europe, with Cook's orchestra and with a band led by drummer Benny Peyton, until 1921. During this sojourn he cut his first records (in London and Paris) and bought his first soprano saxophone. Saxophones were a novelty to jazz players in those days, and soprano saxophones doubly so. Bechet became enamored of the soprano sax, however, and played it with increasing frequency in the early 1920s, until eventually he gave up the clarinet almost entirely.

Upon his return from Europe, Bechet made his first recordings, including some on soprano saxophone, with New Orleans pianist Clarence Williams's Blue Five. He played for short spells in various revues and jazz bands—among them, Duke Ellington's and pianist James P. Johnson's. Then, in 1925 or 1926, he returned to Europe, playing in the U.S.S.R., Germany, France, and The Netherlands. Bechet returned to the United

States in 1931, and during the 1930s he worked for bandleader Noble Sissle (with whom he had played in France), rejoined Duke Ellington, organized the New Orleans Footwarmers with New Orleans/Chicago trumpeter Tommy Ladnier, played once again with Sissle, and with Zutty Singleton and stride pianist Willie "The Lion" Smith, and performed with his old teachers, Lorenzo Tio and George Baquet. Throughout the 1940s, he played in top jazz clubs in New York and other Eastern cities, and in 1949 and 1950 he toured Europe again.

In 1951, Bechet settled more or less permanently in France, where he became a celebrity whose constituency (like Louis Armstrong's in the United States) far exceeded conventional jazz audiences. He recorded with many top French traditional and swing jazz musicians, including the fine Algerian-born neo-bop pianist Martial Solal, and with a host of American expatriate jazz artists. In addition, he traveled widely, to play and to record. Bechet was active in jazz until his death. One of his last appearances was in 1958, when he led an all-star jazz group at the World's Fair in Brussels.

The sounds Bechet made with his new instrument were quite unique to jazz, and they remained his alone for some time to come. Bechet played with a fearless attack and a broad vibrato, and his tone has an edge to it that is positively riveting. He took the New Orleans reed tradition, with its considerable virtues of fluidity and warmth, and added sharpness and depth. Although other musicians took up the soprano sax in later years (most notably Bechet's protégé Bob Wilber and the superb player Steve Lacy), it was not until John Coltrane's recordings in the early 1960s that jazz gained another truly brilliant voice on soprano saxophone.

Selected Recordings

Sidney Bechet with Clarence Williams and His Blue Five (Swaggy)
The Blue Bechet (RCA)
Sidney Bechet Jazz Classics (two volumes, Blue Note)
Sidney Bechet Volume 1 (Vogue)
Le Soir où l'on cassa l'Olympia (two-record set) (Vogue)

The album with Williams and His Blue Five, on the Australian Swaggy label, includes some of the earliest Bechet recordings, from 1921, when he was just back from Europe. *Blue Bechet* dates from 1939–40 and features pianists Earl Hines and Willie "The Lion" Smith, among others. The Blue Note albums are from about the same period and feature pianists like Art Hodes and boogie-woogie wizard Meade Lux Lewis. The first of the two albums on the French Vogue label matches Bechet with the dazzling French pianist Martial Solal, a versatile musician best-known for his excursions into the quasi–avant-garde. The second, whose title might be translated as "The Night They Broke Up the Olympia" (a popular French concert hall), is performed with the solid French swing bands of Claude Luter and André Réwéliotty.

n 1917, the Secretary of the Navy, worried about the moral and physical well-being of his young seafaring charges, obtained a government order closing the brothels in New Orleans' Storyville district. The budding jazz musicians of the city, abruptly deprived of their favorite audiences, assembled in the streets that very afternoon and marched, to a ragtime beat, straight down to the levee, where they hopped forthwith on anything that would float and cruised apace straight up the Mississippi River to St. Louis. From there, they scrambled overland, their instruments in tow, to the banks of Lake Michigan, to Chicago, and to points east, thereby spreading jazz into the heartland and lifeblood of America, and eventually into the world at large.

That colorful story is the impression given by some versions of the northward migration of jazz. There are, however, a few things wrong with such accounts. To begin with, the Secretary of the Navy did close New Orleans' brothels in 1917, but jazz had not been whorehouse music, and jazz musicians had rarely found employ in Storyville. (Those that had were mostly pianists, whose choice of instrument excluded them from street bands, and occasional vocalists.) More to the point, some pioneer jazz musicians (Eubie Blake, for instance) were not even in New Orleans in the first place, and others had already left the city by the time Storyville was shuttered. There was a massive northward emigration of blacks of all professions (including, presumably, musicians) in those years; the black population of Chicago more than doubled between 1910 and 1920.

Even before 1917, jazz had a firm foothold in many cities beyond New Orleans. Before the fateful crackdown, Fate Marable was already well-known to St. Louis audiences, and clarinetist Lawrence Duhé played in a band that included Lil Hardin on Chicago's South Side in 1916. A white group called The Original Dixieland Jass [sic] Band (which as Brown's Dixieland Jass Band had played in Chicago in 1915), opened at Reisenweber's Restaurant on Columbus Circle in New York City early in 1917, before the New Orleans brothel ban. The band was such a sensation that they were soon making an unheard-of $1,000 a week. This group—Nick LaRocca on cornet, Larry Shields on clarinet, Eddie Edwards on trombone, Harry Ragas on piano, and Tony Sbarbara (or Spargo) on drums—made the first jazz recording ever (also in 1917). The record consisted of "Livery Stable Blues," on which the cornet and trombone imitated barnyard animals, and "Dixieland Jass Band One-Step," neither of which offered much in the way of improvisation. (The disk is said eventually to have sold a million copies.)

In the years after 1915 and the early 1920s, Chicago became the new first city of jazz—the place where jazz took shape and where its best practitioners came together to develop their voices. If jazz was raised in New Orleans, so to speak, it went to high school in Chicago.

Jazz historian Frederic Ramsey, Jr., estimates that by 1920, there were more than forty top New Orleans jazz musicians in Chicago. Among these, certainly, were King Oliver, Johnny Dodds, Jimmie Noone, Honoré Dutrey, trumpeter Natty Dominique, drummer Minor "Ram" Hall, and such groups as the Original Dixieland Jass Band and the New Orleans Rhythm Kings. By 1930, most jazz performers of any consequence had played there for at least one extended engagement.

Of course, jazz did not stop in Chicago. Before moving to that city in 1925, Kid Ory had gone to California for his health, and he spent about half a dozen years there, bringing jazz to Los Angeles, San Francisco, and Oakland—becoming, in Los Angeles in 1921, the first black jazz performer to make a record. Sidney Bechet went to London and Paris, and the Original Dixieland Jass Band to London. King Oliver, Jelly Roll Morton, and, later, the first great white jazz musician, Bix Beiderbecke, took their music across Indiana from Chicago to the Gennett recording studios in Richmond, and Gennett brought it to the world. Colorado-born bandleader Paul Whiteman, with Beiderbecke as his star, introduced New York to the refined side of jazz. A young man from Atlanta, Fletcher Henderson, went to New York to study chemistry and ended up creating the first real jazz big band.

Most important, by 1930 jazz was old enough and had been heard enough, in person and especially on records, to have produced a strong second generation of performers. Some of these people had not yet been born when Buddy Bolden, the "first" jazz musician, was remanded to East Louisiana State Hospital. Now musicians like Coleman Hawkins, Ben Webster, Benny Carter, Roy Eldridge, and Lionel Hampton, who were to become the stars of the swing era and beyond, were sitting on bandstands with their pioneer elders, playing hard and well already and probably thinking about where to take jazz next.

BIX BEIDERBECKE *(Leon Bix Beiderbecke) (1903–31)*

Bix Beiderbecke ("Bix" was a given name and not a nickname), born into a conservative upper-middle-class family in Davenport, Iowa, was the first important white jazz musician and is one of the fifteen or twenty best and most influential jazz musicians of all time. The founders of jazz had almost all been black, and early popular white groups had been imitators, not innovators.

Beiderbecke was a self-taught musician, both on piano (on which he started picking out tunes at the age of 5 or 6) and cornet (on which he reportedly forced himself to learn Nick LaRocca solos, note for note, from records). He played in high school bands and then in lesser known professional orchestras in Iowa and Illinois. In 1923, he joined The Wolverines, a jazz/ dance band patterned after the suave white ensemble, The New

Orleans Rhythm Kings. In 1925, he joined forces with Frankie Trumbauer, known as "Tram," whose instrument was the C-melody saxophone. Trumbauer was a technically capable musician, although he seems to have improvised very little; he had a unique tone, very direct and very confident, and later masters of the saxophone like Benny Carter and Johnny Hodges listened very closely to him. Bix and Trumbauer became a team, working together first in Trumbauer's own band, and then with Jean Goldkette (whose orchestra included Tommy and Jimmy Dorsey, violinist Joe Venuti, and guitarist Eddie Lang), and finally with Paul Whiteman, the self-styled "King of Jazz."

Whiteman's orchestra, unquestionably the most popular and famous "jazz" group of its time, and one that did a tremendous amount to further the public consciousness of this new music in America, at the same time had relatively little to do with real jazz. Nevertheless, real jazz musicians, including Venuti and Lang, Jack Teagarden, trumpeter Bunny Berigan, and cornetist Red Nichols, played with Whiteman over the years. Whiteman's orchestra presented jazz-flavored music in a concert setting, including the premiere of Gershwin's "Rhapsody in Blue" in 1924. Whether the solos that Beiderbecke and other jazzmen played with Whiteman were jazz or not is open to debate, but they certainly owed much to jazz, and, as some of Beiderbecke's work in that context demonstrates, they could certainly be beautiful music.

While with Whiteman, Beiderbecke became increasingly interested in the piano and composed some piano pieces of more than passing interest. The best and most famous of them, which he recorded himself as a piano solo, was "In a Mist"—one of the most durable classics jazz has produced.

Beiderbecke drank heavily and was in bad health for most of his adult life. He left Whiteman in 1929 and was only intermittently active after that until his death from lobar pneumonia and the effects of alcoholism.

Despite his lack of formal training, Beiderbecke had become a formidable cornetist by his Whiteman days. His style was fast and clean, with a rich and attractively brassy tone. More importantly, though, his playing bore virtually no resemblance to that of the great black cornetists who had come before him, and he had a vivid improvisatory imagination that was without obvious antecedent. He was a true original.

Selected Recordings

Bix Beiderbecke and the Wolverines (Riverside)
The Bix Beiderbecke Legend (RCA)
The Bix Beiderbecke Story (three volumes, Columbia)

The Wolverines were one of the best early white jazz bands, and Beiderbecke shines forth on the Riverside recording with such favorites of the day as "Tiger Rag" and "Royal Garden Blues." The RCA album includes Beiderbecke with the Jean Goldkette Orchestra, with Hoagy Carmichael, and with Paul Whiteman.

But the Columbia set is the definitive Beiderbecke collection. The first volume is Bix and his "gang," including bass saxophonist Adrian Rollini on some tracks. The second is Bix with Frankie Trumbauer, with guitarist Eddie Lang and clarinetist Jimmy Dorsey participating on some tracks. The third volume is mostly classic Bix with Paul Whiteman.

FLETCHER HENDERSON   *(James Fletcher Henderson)*

(1898–1952)

Fletcher Henderson studied classical piano for most of his childhood but didn't anticipate a musical career. He studied chemistry at Atlanta University College and moved to New York in 1920 to further his studies. He abandoned academic life soon thereafter and went to work for a series of music publishing and recording companies as a song demonstrator, recording manager, and house pianist. He recorded as piano accompanist to blues singers like Bessie Smith, Ida Cox, Alberta Hunter, and Ma Rainey. He formed his own band in 1923, playing mostly blues and pop songs at first, then drifting gradually toward jazz. He was decisively a jazz musician by late 1924, when Louis Armstrong joined his band.

The early band had ten or eleven pieces and featured musicians like saxophonist Coleman Hawkins, clarinetist Buster Bailey, and saxophonist/arranger Don Redman. In time, it grew to about sixteen pieces, developing into the first big band to play real jazz. The band reached its first peak in 1927 and 1928. It went through major personnel changes over the years but remained a strong performing (and recording) unit until 1939, when Henderson broke up the band and went to work for Benny Goodman as a pianist and arranger. The band's lengthy stays at Connie's Inn in Harlem in 1931 and at the Grand Terrace in Chicago in 1936 were particularly noteworthy. Many musicians of subsequent great repute were members of the Henderson band in these years, including (in addition to those mentioned above) trumpeters Rex Stewart, Tommy Ladnier, Roy Eldridge, and Red Allen; trombonists J. C. Higginbotham, Keg Johnson, Dickie Wells, and Benny Morten; saxophonists Benny Carter, Hilton Jefferson, Ben Webster, and Chu Berry; and drummer "Big Sid" Catlett.

Between 1939 and 1950, Henderson did some arranging for Goodman and other bandleaders and led his own groups from 1939 until 1950, when he suffered a stroke that left him an invalid for the rest of his life.

Henderson was never noted as a great pianist, but he was an excellent arranger, for his own bands and for others. Moreover, he helped to establish what became the standard swing band jazz style—his influence on the later white pop/swing bands was immense—and to expose innumerable people to the talented musicians who worked for him and to jazz itself.

Selected Recordings

Fletcher Henderson and the Connie's Inn Orchestra (RCA)
Fletcher Henderson: A Study in Frustration (four volumes, Columbia)
The Immortal Fletcher Henderson (Milestone)

The RCA LP dates from 1931 and includes Coleman Hawkins and Rex Stewart in what was one of Henderson's better, more cohesive bands. The four-volume Columbia set is an invaluable documentation not only of Henderson's work throughout most of his career, but of an entire period of jazz history: it shows off to good advantage Hawkins, Stewart, Roy Eldridge, and countless other musicians who were to become important figures in the swing era and offers a vivid view of the changes in big-band swing from the early 1920s to the late 1930s. The Milestone album represents what many think was the Henderson band's finest period, around 1927–28. Trombonist Benny Morton, trumpeter Tommy Ladnier, clarinetist Buster Bailey, and others are present and in excellent form, and the band plays with great force and unity of purpose.

-3-

Ragtime, Stride, and Boogie-Woogie

There is a style of music—and more specifically a style of piano playing—that predated jazz and was one of the most important contributors to the development of jazz. It was virtually synonymous with jazz in its early years and has existed in recognizable form in jazz to this day. The style is ragtime. It grew into stride piano (sometimes known at first as "Harlem piano"), and its basic musical principles can be identified in composers and performers from Scott Joplin to Thelonious Monk and beyond, including such giants of the jazz piano as James P. Johnson, Fats Waller, Earl Hines, Teddy Wilson, and Art Tatum.

The piano is the only important jazz instrument that can either accompany itself or play with other instruments as either an accompaniment or a strong solo instrument. Moreover, it can play both the figure and the ground. This latter ability, most of all, has been the key element in the birth and longevity of ragtime and stride.

Ragtime

Ragtime probably emerged as a popular piano style in the 1880s, although its greatest period of prominence ran from about 1895 to 1917 or 1918. At first, it was a kind of party music, and sometimes dance music. Later, it was also presented in concert settings and was adopted as a widely applicable device by the songwriters of Tin Pan Alley. It was a very precise music, lending itself easily to conventional musical notation, and, despite its cultural origins, it had little to do with the blues.

Ragtime is a relentlessly syncopated music whose simplest form consists of spare, right-hand melodic lines played eight beats to the measure and accented on the first, fourth, and seventh beats, thrown against a plain, sometimes almost plodding left-hand rhythmic line played four beats to the measure and accented on the first and third beats.

Good ragtime is full of shifting accents and rhythmic quirks of many kinds and often characterized by extremely beautiful, elegant melodies. Furthermore, as it spread and was taken up by various musicians (most frequently in New Orleans, at the outset, and then in New York), ragtime became looser, more lilting, even more bluesy. It started to swing.

The first important composer of ragtime was Scott Joplin, whose work (especially "Maple Leaf Rag") has long been popular but whose name first became generally familiar when his music was adapted for use in the motion picture called "The Sting." Joplin was born in Texas but he spent his professional life in Missouri and, later, in New York. He published his first compositions in 1895, when he was 27. He was a prolific composer not only of ragtime music but also of other popular forms, and he wrote two operas.

Jelly Roll Morton was a key figure in jazz from its New Orleans period until the birth of swing. Born in the mid-1880s, he knew ragtime music well, incorporated many elements of ragtime into his playing, and sometimes played ragtime itself, along with the blues and other less inhibited musical forms. Like many other ragtime and stride pianists, Morton was a true character: one of the comparatively few important jazz figures who really did play for some time in the brothels of New Orleans, he was an eccentric, a dandy, and a fancy talker. He also had an extraordinarily high regard for his own talents. Appraisals of his value to jazz are mixed (Duke Ellington, for one, is said to have considered him a phony). Still, intimations of his exuberant, colorful style can be heard in many later pianists.

Morton's contemporary, Eubie Blake has been tremendously popular as a songwriter: "Memories of You" and "I'm Just Wild About Harry" were extremely popular in their day. He also has written and played a very sophisticated brand of ragtime, the most obvious immediate ancestor of the stride piano style.

Stride

Stride took the rhythmic principles of ragtime and transposed them. Stride was jaunty music: the bass loped rather than marched; melody was embellished. A whole range of European piano and orchestral techniques, many of them involving dynamics, were introduced into the music, sometimes skillfully and sometimes naïvely and imprecisely. Most of all, although the figure and the ground were still strongly apparent, the distance between them began to increase. The listener still had the firm, heavy bass line to hold onto, but the melody went its own way now and again.

The father of stride piano was James P. Johnson, who had been influenced by both Blake and Morton. With his fellow New Yorker, Willie "The Lion" Smith, Johnson elaborated on the advanced ragtime of his imaginative predecessors and passed on the stride tradition to other, younger musicians—the most noteworthy being Thomas "Fats" Waller.

Waller studied with Johnson, both formally and informally, and proved to be an exciting pianist, a superb composer ("Honeysuckle Rose," "Squeeze Me," and "Ain't Misbehavin'" are among his most famous songs), and, eventually, a well-known entertainer. Waller was an engaging vocalist, who became famous in non-jazz circles for his affectionate parodies of current popular hits, but he was also a major jazz figure. He was the first musician to use the organ seriously as a jazz instrument, and brought tenderness and what might be called contemplativeness to stride piano.

Boogie-Woogie

As Johnson, Smith, Waller, and others were refining stride piano, another kind of piano playing was becoming popular. Dubbed "boogie-woogie," this new piano style seemed at first to be a relative of ragtime and early stride—mostly because of the persuasiveness of its bass line and the way its bass rhythm and treble melody played against each other. In fact, it was a much more primitive kind of music, with a different set of ancestors—guitar and piano blues traditions and the ebullient "barrel-house" piano of the Southern bars and brothels—and no progeny to speak of.

Musically, boogie-woogie was a rephrasing of the blues and was characterized by a bass line played eight beats to the bar.

Boogie-woogie technique has been described as "trilling the treble and rolling the bass," and the best practitioners of the style could keep that rolling bass flowing with formidable sure-footedness while scattering little runs and grace notes all over the upper end of the keyboard.

Earl "Fatha" Hines was a both great amalgamator of piano styles and an innovator in his own right. A serious student of classical piano as a child, he was well versed in pure ragtime, was heavily influenced by Fats Waller, and was endowed with a fine understanding of the same blues traditions that gave shape to boogie-woogie. Going beyond these forms, he freed jazz piano from the strictures of the earlier music and created what has been called the "trumpet style" of piano playing, with a right hand that played free-flying, brassy-clean runs similar to what a trumpet might play.

Hines broke ground for the better stride-influenced pianists of the late 1930s and 1940s. Among these were Jess Stacy, Mel Powell, Art Hodes (who was really more of a blues player), and, most important, Teddy Wilson—who was easily the most imitated pianist of the swing era and remains one of the most re-fined players that jazz has ever had. The last great jazz pianist whose work was unmistakably a continuation of stride was Art Tatum, a spectacular technician whose speed and precision stunned other pianists along with his audiences. Tatum intro-duced new ideas about harmony and rhythm into jazz piano, but his debt to Waller and Hines is easily apparent.

JAMES P. JOHNSON *(1891–1955)*

Born in New Jersey and brought up there and in New York, James P. Johnson had virtually no direct exposure to the black Southern roots of jazz and ap-parently first heard the music the same way that most Americans did: through the Original Dixie-land Jass Band.

Johnson's mother was a pian-ist, and he learned to play the in-strument from her. He took to it naturally and soon developed a budding career for himself, play-ing ragtime, dance tunes, music hall hits, and other kinds of pop-ular music suited to the piano. He performed first at Coney Is-land and later in Manhattan and Atlantic City—the latter of which was a regular summer showcase for black entertainers.

As Johnson heard more and more jazz ideas, he started bringing them into his playing. He also seemed to have an in-tuitive feeling for the blues and became one of Bessie Smith's more important accompanists. While he was developing his own piano style—which was to become stride piano—he was also becoming a versatile composer. Before his career was ended by a stroke in 1951, he had composed music for a number of other shows, a large number of jazz and pop songs, among them, "Charleston," and serious works, including symphonies, ballet scores, operettas, tone poems, and a piano concerto.

For most of Johnson's career, he was much in demand as an accompanist and a band pianist, and in the early 1940s, after recovering from his first stroke, he worked in small groups with cornetist Wild Bill Davison, guitarist Eddie Condon, and, later, clarinetist Albert Nicholas.

Johnson took ragtime a great distance from its rather staid origins. He was less than a star during his lifetime, but his musical ideas have shone through jazz.

Selected Recordings

The Original James P. Johnson (Folkways)
Father of the Stride Piano (Biograph)
Nobody's Blues But Mine by Bessie Smith (two-record set, Columbia)

The Folkways recordings are of fairly good, representative solo work in the 1940s and are clear examples of Johnson's stride style. *Father . . .* is splendid and includes small-band recordings with musicians like trombonist J. C. Higginbotham and the great drummer Big Sid Catlett, some particularly rousing solo work, and a duet with pianist Clarence Williams, vintage 1930. The Bessie Smith record includes several tracks showing Johnson off to good advantage as an accompanist.

EARL "FATHA" HINES *(1905–   )*

Earl Hines came from a musical family and studied piano from an early age. Majoring in music at a Pittsburgh high school, he was discovered by singer/saxophonist Lois Deppe, and was hired to join Deppe's band. Hines developed his unique piano style while touring with Deppe.

The same year, Hines settled in Chicago, where he managed to play with most of the important New Orleans musicians of the time, including Louis Armstrong, Jimmie Noone, Johnny Dodds, and Sidney Bechet. Some solo piano records made in 1928 for the Q.R.S. company attracted great attention in the jazz community, as did a big band that he formed late in the same year.

Throughout the 1930s and 1940s (until 1947), Hines led bands in Chicago and New York and on tour, taking into his fold such young bop players as Charlie Parker and Dizzy Gillespie. In 1948, Hines joined Louis Armstrong's All-Stars. In 1951, he formed his own small group, and then continued to lead his own ensembles and to play in a number of high-quality pick-up bands for various tours and festivals. He still has not officially retired, and still is playing with a vigor that is remarkable in a man of his age.

Hines's famous "trumpet style" piano lines were a landmark in the development of jazz keyboard playing, challenging ideas believed to be sacred about the relationship of the piano's treble and bass, and coincidentally anticipating some important facets of bop piano playing; it is tremendous fun to listen to.

Selected Recordings

Famous QRS Solos (Atlantic)
The Fatha Jumps (two-record set, RCA)
Louis Armstrong in Canada by Louis Armstrong (two-record set, Dogwood)
Earl "Fatha" Hines Plays Duke Ellington (four volumes, Master Jazz)

The Atlantic album offers Hines' 1928 recordings for the Q.R.S. label. The RCA set features the 14-piece Hines big band in various versions. The Armstrong album shows Hines off to excellent advantage, along with Jack Teagarden and Barney Bigard. The Ellington tributes, from the early 1970s, are superb solo pieces, especially Volume One.

ART TATUM   *(1910–56)*

Blind in one eye and partially blind in the other since birth, Art Tatum attended both a school for the blind and a school of music as a child in his native Ohio. He formed his first band when he was about 16, and by the time he was 22, he was good enough to be hired as accompanist to the noted vocalist Adelaide Hall, who brought him to New York.

Almost as soon as Tatum left Adelaide Hall's employ, he developed a formidable reputation as a piano soloist, not only with audiences, but among his fellow musicians, some of whom considered him the greatest jazz pianist who had ever lived. There is a story that Fats Waller was playing in a club in Chicago one night, when he looked down

24 Ragtime, Stride, and Boogie-Woogie

and recognized Tatum listening to him. "Ladies and gentlemen," Waller is said to have announced, "I play piano—but God is in the house tonight."

Throughout the 1930s and early 1940s, Tatum worked regularly in New York, Cleveland, and Chicago. He also toured Europe and settled on the West Coast for a time. He almost always worked as a soloist during these years, but in 1943, he formed a trio with guitarist Tiny Grimes and bassist Slam Stewart. He also did most of his later performing as part of a trio, although the personnel changed from time to time. In the years before his death, he was recorded frequently, both as a soloist and teamed with a goodly variety of other prominent musicians, by impresario Norman Granz—a blessing for those of us who can know Tatum only through his records.

Tatum was a virtuoso: he embellished lines shamelessly; he turned chord changes inside out, knocked them down, and rebuilt them in a new style. He could scatter familiar melodies in all directions and somehow make them all come back together again in recognizable form.

Tatum might be said to have been a precursor of bop because of the way he fastened onto mediocre tunes and transformed them into complicated reinterpretations of their former selves, and, more important, the way he relentlessly questioned accepted principles of improvisation and worked unceasingly to find new ways to build with old materials. He has certainly inspired other pianists by his matchless brilliance in reaching for excellence and daring to try new things.

Selected Recordings

Art Tatum Masterpieces, Volume One (two-record set, MCA)
Solo Piano (Capitol)
The Tatum Solo Masterpieces (thirteen volumes or thirteen-record set, Pablo)
The Tatum Group Masterpieces: Art Tatum/Ben Webster (Pablo)

The MCA set, part of a series presented by jazz critic Leonard Feather, includes ample representations of first-rate Tatum solo and trio recordings from throughout the 1930s, and even includes some tracks with blues shouter Joe Turner. The Capitol LP dates from 1949, and offers excellent short solo versions of sixteen standards. In its entirety the Pablo set contains some 121 selections, mostly from 1953 and 1954. The entire production is for Tatum fanatics only, but any volume or two would enrich any record collection. (Volume Three, with its delicate reinterpretation of Fats Waller's "Jitterbug Waltz" would be a good place to start.) The Webster album, part of another multi-volume Pablo set, also shows the pianist playing with such fine swing-era musicians as trumpeter Roy Eldridge and vibraharpist Lionel Hampton, and is a real delight, with Tatum's harmonic complexity playing superbly against Webster's richly textured, deceptively straightforward tenor saxophone.

–4–
The Swing Era

The swing era may have been born in 1928, when Jelly Roll Morton's Red Hot Peppers recorded "Georgia Swing" and "Kansas City Stomp." Perhaps it started in 1929, on one of those many nights when Bennie Moten's band (or was it Walter Page's Blue Devils?) got an entire Kansas City ballroom jumping, roof and all. Of course, there are also those who say that the swing era began in 1932, when Duke Ellington recorded the anthem of the idiom, "It Don't Mean a Thing (If It Ain't Got That Swing)" with such luminaries as Johnny Hodges, Barney Bigard, Harry Carney, and the underrated Otto (Toby) Hardwicke in his saxophone section—sax being an all-important element in swing. Maybe it was in 1934, when the Dorsey brothers, trombonist Tommy and saxophonist/clarinetist Jimmy, established the great swing band, with arrangements by Glenn Miller, that defined the music for young white America. One thing is certain: by mid-1936, when the Onyx Club in New York City presented a "Swing Music Concert" (featuring the likes of Artie Shaw, Tommy Dorsey, and Bob Crosby), swing had arrived.

Defining Swing

What *is* swing? The answer gets a bit complicated, because it is necessary first to differentiate between swing music, the popular/jazz music dating from somewhere around the late 1920s or early 1930s to the mid-1940s (and later imitations or reconstructions of it), and music that swings—which might be swing music but might also be ragtime, hard bop, or Strauss waltzes.

To swing, in musical parlance, is to play with a certain elusive rhythmic sense—a sense that implies a kind of slight skewing of metrical continuity in a way that cannot be expressed in musical notation. It is an interpretive trick. Stanley Dance, who has written on Duke Ellington and the swing era, has proposed that swing "is an exhilarating rhythmic feeling created around a fundamental pulse that suggests—but does not actually realize—a quickening of tempo." This might be true, but swing also involves a slight rhythmic hesitation. It is a matter of rhythmic control: there is something insistent, even compelling, about music that swings. In other words, swing defies neat definitions.

There was much more to swing music than simply "swinging." As the popularity of jazz spread, many strains developed and cross-pollinated each other. The roots of jazz—including ragtime and blues—emerged again and again: regional forms of jazz met head-on and turned into cosmopolitan varieties; and somewhere along the line, the rhythmic certainty of stride piano met up with the blues-rich riff bands of the Southwest and the mannered concert bands of Chicago and the Northeast. Swing was born.

The Big Bands

For the most part, swing was big-band music, although there were certainly exceptions like some of Benny Goodman's small bands or bassist John Kirby's legendary swing sextet. In New Orleans and in the first years of the jazz diaspora, "big" bands numbered eight or nine pieces. By the late 1920s, the thirteen-to sixteen-piece big band of modern times had become commonplace, bringing with it a tonal authority and an improvisational versatility jazz had never known before. The larger groups lent themselves naturally to strong rhythms and to the nagging, almost hypnotic riffs that propelled so much swing music. These bands were the perfect laboratory for at least a tentative mixing of what had become the two main streams of jazz—the "hot" and the "sweet"—expressed in big swing bands by the blistering, shouting soloists and the mellow, sometimes muted ensemble sounds of the reed and brass sections.

The great swing bands included all of those mentioned and also those led by Luis Russell, Earl Hines, Jimmy Lunceford, Andy Kirk, Harlan Leonard, Claude Hopkins, Chick Webb, Don Redman, Benny Carter, Bunny Berigan, Charlie Barnet, Harry James, Woody Herman, Lionel Hampton (the latter two somewhat later in the swing era), and the great Count Basie. They toured endlessly and played ceaselessly, performing exciting music that was both amiable and forceful. With swing, jazz came the closest it has ever come to being a truly "popular" musical form. Swing, as a cultural phenomenon at least, was the rock-and-roll of its time. It was the music that "no-good" teenagers danced to, the music whose implications (hot parties, hard booze, "Negro" rhythms) were denounced by the older generation and embraced by the younger.

Arranging Swing

Because it was big-band music, swing was also arrangers' music. Great soloists came out of the swing era, to be sure—Goodman, Coleman Hawkins, Lester Young, and Roy Eldridge chief among them—but the sound of swing was the sound of the bands, and the bands had identities that were the work of the arrangers, who translated popular songs or relatively simple jazz ideas into complex, many-sided voicings for large numbers of musicians. Some of these arrangers had been, were, or soon became noted bandleaders and/or musicians on their own— among them, Fletcher Henderson and his brother Horace, Claude Hopkins, Benny Carter, Don Redman, Glenn Miller, Luis Russell, Mary Lou Williams, and Billy May. Others like Van Alexander, Andy Gibson, Ed Wilcox, Dave Matthews, Edgar Sampson, Fred Norman, Nat Pierce, and the great Billy Strayhorn (who became almost as important to the sound of the Duke Ellington orchestra as Ellington himself was) remained known mainly as arrangers. All of these, and many more, were essential to the character of swing.

Swing was also largely saxophone music. Despite the fact that it was reasonably common in the early years of the century in New Orleans as a band instrument, the saxophone didn't really become a jazz instrument until the early 1920s with Sidney Bechet, Bud Freeman, Frankie Trumbauer, and Adrian Rollini. By the time the great swing bands started appearing, the saxophone had become an integral part of any large-scale jazz instrumentation. The wide range of saxophones available (soprano, alto, tenor, baritone, and bass were the usual ones) encouraged formation of three-, four-, or five-man reed sections, and saxophones in general seemed well suited to the new music. Playing together, in harmony, they could sound sweet and warm: as solo instruments they could, when necessary, be rough and searing.

Swing was, finally, one other thing: almost by its very nature, it was music you could dance to; and good swing was music you couldn't *not* dance to. America before the Second World War was dance-crazy, and the big bands' best venue was the dancehall. In a sense, this was swing's downfall: it grew too sweet, too polished, too highly stylized, and the dancing took precedence over the playing. It is perhaps extreme to say that swing forsook its roots, but it certainly grew far away from them in some cases, and cooled down by the early 1940s.

BENNIE MOTEN   *(1894–1935)*

Bennie Moten was a child of Kansas City, but a father of the Kansas City jazz style—the two-beat, blues-rich, hard-swinging music that is familiar to most listeners today primarily through the work of New Jerseyite Count Basie. Moten's mother played piano, and his own first musical engagement came when he was 12 and signed on with a juvenile brass band to play baritone horn. He switched to piano and played with local groups as a teenager; and in the early 1920s, he formed his own small group and gradually built it into a big band. He had few periods of inactivity from that time until his premature death, and he gave important early jobs to fine musicians like trumpeter Hot Lips Page, bassist Walter Page (who became an important bandleader himself), saxophonists Ben Webster and Buster Smith, and Count Basie.

Moten was a tireless exponent of Kansas City blues and swing who played all over the Midwest and East. At times he had more than one band under his name playing simultaneously, a practice not uncommon at the time. He was a solid but undistinguished pianist and a fine arranger in what was admittedly a rather basic style, but he was most important for his talent as a bandleader, as a champion of his music, and for the fact that Count Basie's first great band grew out of the remnants of his.

Selected Recordings

Bennie Moten's Kansas City Orchestra (Historical Records)
Count Basie in Kansas City (RCA)

The Historical Records material is mostly early, heavily blues-influenced material (including "South," "Vine Street Blues," and others) by a medium-sized band, and is a good example of the more elementary Kansas City style. The Count Basie recordings are from 1930 to 1932, when Moten had what was probably his strongest, most sophisticated group, featuring not only Basie (on second piano), but Ben Webster, Buster Smith, Hot Lips Page, and blues shouter Jimmy Rushing.

COUNT BASIE   *(William Basie) (1904–   )*

Count Basie—given his sobriquet as a promotional gimmick in 1935, in Kansas City—played drums as a child but picked up piano rudiments at an early age from his pianist mother. He took lessons on organ from Fats Waller as a teenager and started playing professionally around New Jersey (where he was born) and New York. During the mid-1920s, most of his work was in vaudeville and variety shows, but after being stranded in Kansas City on a tour in 1927 and working for a time as a theatre organist, he joined Walter Page's Blue Devils, which led him directly, in 1929, to Bennie Moten's orchestra.

Basie remained with Moten until 1934, when he left to head one of the splinter bands that Moten had working for him. He returned to·the main band the next year and remained with the group after Moten's death in 1935. Later that year, Basie went off to found his own band, a small group that grew gradually into a big one and came to include many of the best players from Page's and Moten's bands. In time Walter Page himself became an essential part of Basie's famous rhythm section, which also included guitarist Freddie Green, drummer Jo Jones, and Basie himself. Jimmy Rushing joined Basie, as did tenor players Lester Young, Herschel Evans, Don Byas, and Buddy Tate; trumpeters Buck Clayton, Joe Newman, and Harry "Sweets" Edison; and trombonists Benny Morton and Dicky Wells.

Basie's early band was heard by John Hammond, a music critic and key figure in the record business since the 1930s. It was he who arranged the Basie band's·first national tour, which included stops at the inevitable Grand Terrace in Chicago and Roseland in New York. By the late 1930s, after hit engagements at the Savoy Ballroom in New York ("The Home of Happy Feet") and other top clubs, Basie's had become one of the most popular bands in America.

Throughout the 1940s, the Basie band worked constantly—on tour, on recording dates, and in films—and Basie himself worked solo engagements and recorded with the Benny Goodman Sextet. In 1950, for economic reasons, he broke up the band temporarily and worked with a septet for about two years. In 1952, he reformed the band. The Basie bands of the 1950s were more sophisticated, more whimsical, and more versatile than the earlier bands had been. Among the excellent musicians who were in the band during this period (though not all at the same time) were Joe Newman and his fellow trumpeters Joe Wilder and Thad Jones, reed players Paul Quinichette, Eddie "Lockjaw" Davis, Frank Foster, Frank Wess, and Marshall Royal, trombonist Bennie Powell, drummer Sonny Payne, and vocalist Joe Williams—plus the all-important Freddie Green.

In the 1960s, the band seemed to lose creative momentum—it certainly lost many key soloists—but Basie continued to hire good players (trombonists Richard Boone and Curtis Fuller, trumpeter Oscar Brashear, and others) and held onto or re-hired some of his old standbys. He is still intermittently active.

Basie is a charming, swinging, highly economical pianist and a composer of some success ("One O'Clock Jump" is his most famous tune), but he is really important as one of the best, most effective leaders of large groups of musicians there has ever been in jazz. He is still playing actively.

Selected Recordings

The First Records He Ever Made (Sandy Hook)
Super Chief (two-record set, Columbia)
The Best of Count Basie (two-record set, MCA)
The Count Basie Story (two-record set, Roulette)
Afrique (Flying Dutchman)
For the First Time (Pablo)

The Sandy Hook Album represents some of Basie's first recorded work as a leader and includes music by a 1936 quintet featuring Lester Young and the 1937 edition of the big band, with Young, Herschel Evans, Buck Clayton, and Jimmy Rushing, among others. Similar groups are included on *Super Chief,* an excellent two-record representation of Basie's work from 1936 to 1942. There are also other small and large groups on the set, an entire side of top Basie soloists with non-Basie bands, and vocal tracks by Billie Holiday, Helen Humes, Jimmy Rushing, and Mildred Bailey. The MCA two-record compilation includes classic big-band versions, from the 1930s and 1940s, of "Jumpin' at the Woodside," "John's Idea," "Cherokee," "Topsy," and others. The Roulette set is a fascinating curiosity—versions of many of the same songs that the MCA set contains, recorded by the 1961 edition of the band (which some observers consider to have been the last really interesting Basie aggregation). The *Afrique* album is intriguing and occasionally stirring, tentatively avant-garde. *For the First Time* presents Basie in an unusual trio context.

COLEMAN HAWKINS *(1904–69)*

Coleman Hawkins was born in St. Joseph, Missouri. At the age of 9, after three years or so of playing piano and cello, he took up the tenor saxophone. He scarcely ever put it down again. He studied music formally at school in Chicago and Topeka, and informally anywhere he could hear it. By the time he was 16, he was playing music professionally on a regular basis— mostly in and around Kansas City. In 1921, blues singer Mamie Smith hired him to join her Jazz Hounds. He attracted some attention in that group, and in 1924 was hired by Fletcher Henderson. He stayed with the Henderson band for ten years and seems to have been profoundly affected by Louis Armstrong's stint with the same organization.

When Hawkins left Henderson in 1934, he was one of the indisputable stars of jazz and was widely considered to be a better saxophonist than even Lester Young. He went to Europe in 1934 and remained there until 1939, playing and recording with bands in England, France, Switzerland, Belgium, The Netherlands, and elsewhere. He returned to the United States at the peak of his powers: a recording he made late in that year of Johnny Green's "Body and Soul" became one of the landmarks of jazz.

After recording "Body and Soul," Hawkins led a big band briefly, then reverted to smaller groups, which he worked with for most of the rest of his life. He was one of the early champions of bop, hiring musicians like pianist Thelonious Monk and trumpeters Dizzy Gillespie, Fats Navarro, and Howard McGhee at a time when most other musicians of Hawkins's generation found these men to be cacophonous upstarts. In the late 1940s and early 1950s, Hawkins toured with Jazz at the Philharmonic and returned several times to Europe. He co-led a strong quintet with trumpeter Roy Eldridge in the early 1950s, toured Europe with tenor saxophonist Illinois Jacquet, recorded frequently with many different groups, appeared on numerous jazz television shows, and performed at almost every important American jazz festival of the decade. He continued to play, mostly in New York and Europe, almost until his death.

Hawkins's sound on tenor was rich and full-bodied, a marked contrast to that of Lester Young. At his best, Hawkins had phenomenal breath control and formidable energy. He was not only a master technician, but also had a fundamental understanding of the bases of music; he could swing mightily and improvise music with great spontaneity, but he was able to be a very "smart" player, too, with his influential flawless tone.

Selected Recordings

A Study in Frustration by Fletcher Henderson (four volumes,
  Columbia)
Body and Soul (RCA)
Monk/Trane (two-record set, Milestone)
The Hawk Flies (Milestone)
Sirius (Pablo)

There are generous representations of Hawkins on the Fletcher
Henderson records, including solos on "Sugarfoot Stomp,"
"My Gal Sal," and "Honeysuckle Rose." The RCA set includes
the original version of "Body and Soul," and "One Hour," on
which Hawkins recorded (backed by a swing group called the
Mound City Blue Blowers) what Leonard Feather says may
well have been "the first genuine jazz ballad solo".

The Hawk Flies is a mixed bag of bop era Hawkins tracks,
including work with Thelonius Monk, trombonist J. J. Johnson,
trumpeter Fats Navarro, and vibraharpist Milt Jackson. *Monk/
Trane* is a 1957 recording of Hawkins with Monk and saxophonist John Coltrane. The Pablo album is an example of
Hawkins's better playing from the mid-1960s, a quartet date
with a new version of "The Man I Love."

LESTER YOUNG   *(1909–59)*

Born into a family of professional musicians in Mississippi and
raised in New Orleans when the
music of King Oliver and Louis
Armstrong was in the air, Young
was taught how to play a number
of instruments (including alto
saxophone) as a youth and first
worked in his father's band as a
drummer. In his early twenties,
he left that group and went to
work touring with a band called
Art Bronson's Bostonians, with
which he played tenor saxophone for the first time.

In the early 1930s, Young
played with bands in and around Minneapolis, joined Bennie
Moten and, briefly, both King Oliver and Fletcher Henderson,
and then became a part of Count Basie's Reno Club combo in
1936. He was one of Basie's star soloists until late 1940. During this period, he recorded with Billie Holiday and formed a
long association with her that was both professional and personal. It is said that it was Holiday who gave Young his nickname, "Prez" or "Pres"—short for "The President," in honor of
his premier position among saxophonists.

Young led his own small groups after leaving Basie, including one with his brother, drummer Lee Young, and joined a big band led by the underrated tenor player, Al Sears, in 1943. Late that year, he temporarily rejoined Basie, then played briefly with Dizzy Gillespie. From December 1943 until September 1944, Young was back with Basie again, until he was inducted into the army, where he spent a year imprisoned for drug possession.

Upon discharge from the army, Young led or played with various small groups of widely varying quality, joined Norman Granz's Jazz at the Philharmonic jam-session tours, and recorded for Granz on the Verve label with fine pianists like Teddy Wilson, Hank Jones, Oscar Peterson, and Nat "King" Cole. By that time, though, literally dozens of other saxophonists were playing the way he did (Wardell Gray and Stan Getz being among the best of these), while his playing was becoming increasingly erratic, with only intermittent touches of his old creative brilliance. His health continued to decline, and he was in and out of hospitals for the last ten years of his life. In early 1959, he played an engagement in Paris; less than twenty-four hours after his return to the United States, he died.

Young once said that his unique style developed because, as a fledgling tenor player, he had tried to emulate Frankie Trumbauer's C-melody saxophone sound on his own B-flat instrument. Whatever the explanation, Young certainly sounded like nobody else. His playing was extremely lithe and strangely delicate (though never weak), with an unusually pure tone. As an improviser, he intuitively anticipated harmonic ideas of the bop and post-bop periods and he was very important to the forward thrust of jazz. This influence has been so pervasive that it may be difficult to hear his performances with fresh ears.

Selected Recordings

The Lester Young Story (four volumes, Columbia)
Lester Young (Commodore)
Pres and Teddy and Oscar (two-record set, Verve)

The four-volume Columbia compilation gives much of the essence of Young's playing from 1936 to 1940, including small groups led by Basie and Benny Goodman, work with vocalists Jimmy Rushing and Billie Holiday, and later big-band material with Basie. The Commodore sessions have superb small-band tracks. They are notable for the presence of the famous Basie rhythm section (Green, Page, and Jones, with Teddy Wilson on piano) and for the fact that Young plays superb clarinet on several tracks. The Verve recordings are arguably the best work that Young did in the 1950s: recordings from 1952 with Oscar Peterson and guitarist Barney Kessel and a 1956 date with Teddy Wilson that includes Young's old friend from Basie days, Jo Jones, on drums.

BENNY GOODMAN *(1909–)*

Benny Goodman is probably the only major jazz figure who can be said to have begun his musical studies in a synagogue. This was at the age of 10. By the time he was 12, he had settled on clarinet as his main instrument and was taking formal musical training at a settlement house in Chicago, his home town. A year later, he was a regular employee of a professional dance band; and by the time he was 16, he was an accomplished musician with more experience than most players in their mid-twenties.

In 1925, when he was 16, Goodman joined drummer Ben Pollack's band, which was considered at the time to be among the best white jazz bands extant, if not the best. He played with Pollack off and on until 1929, when he left the band in New York and began a prolific career of freelance recording and work with bands on the stage and radio. In 1934, he formed his first big band to play at Billy Rose's Music Hall in New York. The Nabisco "Let's Dance" radio show was broadcast coast to coast from Billy Rose's, and Goodman's was one of the featured bands.

In 1935, Goodman took his band on a nationwide tour. It was a fiasco at first: Goodman's band was always the last feature on "Let's Dance," and Eastern and Midwestern audiences had mostly gone to bed by the time it came on. Nevertheless, Goodman pushed on to the West Coast, where people had been listening to and enjoying the band and were eagerly anticipating his arrival. There, at the Palomar Ballroom in Los Angeles, the band was a smash success, and Goodman was launched on his career as one of the world's best-known jazz musicians.

Also in 1935, Goodman formed a trio with pianist Teddy Wilson and drummer Gene Krupa; in 1936, vibraharpist Lionel Hampton joined them, making it a quartet. This was one of the most famous and best small bands of the swing era. In 1938, Goodman and a host of guest stars staged a spectacular all-star concert at Carnegie Hall, and in 1939, he organized the first of his sextets, featuring guitarist Charlie Christian (who virtually invented amplified jazz guitar). Throughout the late 1930s and the 1940s, Goodman led a number of fine big and small bands that included such sidemen as saxophonists Vido Musso, Bud Freeman, and Georgie Auld, trumpeters Harry James, Ziggy Elman, Bunny Berrigan, and Cootie Williams, and pianists Jess Stacy and Mel Powell.

During the same period, Goodman and his band had prominent roles in numerous films, including *Hollywood Hotel, The Big Broadcast of 1937,* and *Stage Door Canteen.* In 1956, Goodman played on the sound track of a film about his life, *The Benny Goodman Story,* starring Steve Allen as Goodman.

Goodman has taken many big and small bands abroad, beginning with an engagement at the London Palladium in 1949. In 1962, he led an excellent big band to the U.S.S.R.—the first American Jazz band to visit that country. Since 1970, he has returned actively to the circuit.

Goodman has also had a minor career as a classical musician. He commissioned and played works for the clarinet by Bartók, Hindemith, and Copland and has performed other clarinet pieces by Mozart, Stravinsky, and Poulenc.

As a composer, Goodman has co-written such jazz standards as "Stompin' at the Savoy," "Lullaby in Rhythm," and "Swingtime in the Rockies." As a clarinetist, he has been a distinct stylist who is perhaps more distinctive in small groups than when playing against a big band but is always technically excellent and astonishingly imaginative. However, his most significant contributions to jazz have been as a leader, both of combos and big bands. He has developed young talents and brought together widely different kinds of players, showing them how to learn from each other. He helped make swing respectable at the same time that he was helping it grow ever more exciting and brought jazz to millions of people who might otherwise never have experienced it.

Selected Recordings

The Golden Age of Swing (five-record set, RCA)
B.G., The Small Groups (RCA)
The Famous 1938 Carnegie Hall Jazz Concert (two-record set, Columbia)
Benny Goodman in Moscow (RCA)
Together Again! (RCA)

The Golden Age of Swing is an extensive, almost exhaustive collection of Goodman big and small groups from the 1930s and 1940s. The RCA small-group material includes trio, quartet, and quintet tracks featuring Krupa, Wilson, Hampton, and others. The Carnegie Hall concert starred Count Basie, Lester Young, Wilson, and Krupa, pianist Jess Stacy, and many others in various configurations, yielding excellent recordings of "One O'Clock Jump," "Sing, Sing, Sing" (with its rudimentary but exquisitely solid solo by Krupa), and other classics. *Benny Goodman in Moscow* includes both sextet and big-band tracks, with Teddy Wilson and vibraharpist Victor Feldman in the former and such luminaries as Joe Newman and Joe Wilder (trumpet), Jimmy Knepper (trombone), Phil Woods and Zoot Sims (reeds), pianist John Bunch, and drummer Mel Lewis in the latter. *Together Again!,* with Wilson, Krupa, and Hampton, is a 1970 reunion of the original quartet.

ROY ELDRIDGE *(David Eldridge) (1911–   )*

Eldridge learned to play drums at the age of 6, then took up the bugle, and finally started playing trumpet (probably around the age of 11 or 12). He left his home in Pittsburgh at 16 to lead a tour band and later played with various carnival and dance bands. In 1928, he went to work for a band led by Horace Henderson and subsequently joined bands led by drummer Speed Webb, multi-instrumentalist Elmer Snowden, reedmen Cecil Scott and Teddy Hill, and pianist Charlie Johnson, among others.

He first came to real prominence, like so many other fine musicians, when he played with Fletcher Henderson (in 1936, in Eldridge's case).

Throughout the rest of the 1930s and the 1940s, Eldridge worked almost continually, leading his own bands and playing as a featured soloist with musicians like Artie Shaw, Benny Goodman, and Gene Krupa, as well as with Jazz at the Philharmonic. He went to Paris with Goodman in 1950 and stayed on by himself for about a year. After he returned to the United States, he played frequently with Coleman Hawkins and clarinetist Sol Yaged, accompanied vocalist Ella Fitzgerald, worked with Count Basie, and continued to lead his own groups. In the early 1970s, he led the house band at Jimmy Ryan's in New York, and he continues to be active.

Eldridge was the best and the most influential of the swing trumpeters and formed an essential bridge between Louis Armstrong and the bop players. There were numerous musicians whose style was molded by his playing—among them, Dizzy Gillespie, whose early recorded playing sounds very Eldridge-like indeed. He was a fast, flashy, brassy player in his heyday, and one who sometimes seemed to think like a saxophonist, not only in the way he constructed his lines, but also in the way he could sound both rough and warm at the same time.

Selected Recordings

A Study in Frustration by Fletcher Henderson (four volumes, Columbia)
Artie Shaw Featuring Roy Eldridge (RCA)
Tour de Force (Verve)
What It's All About (Pablo)

Again, the Henderson collection has pertinent material. The

Shaw material features a particularly spirited long track called "Little Jazz" (Eldridge's nickname). *Tour de Force* is a pleasant, if high-pitched, session featuring Eldridge with fellow trumpeters Dizzy Gillespie and Harry "Sweets" Edison. The Pablo LP is recent material, relaxed and rather happy, featuring reedmen Budd Johnson and Norris Turney.

BENNY CARTER   *(1907–   )*

Two of his cousins were noted professional musicians, and his parents were devoted amateur ones, so Benny Carter, born in New York City, naturally took up music at an early age—piano first, then C-melody saxophone, and then alto saxophone, which became one of his two principal instruments. The other instrument, which he started playing somewhat later, was trumpet. As one of the few jazz musicians who has successfully played both a reed and a brass instrument, Carter stands out.   Carter's first real professional engagement, on alto, came in 1924, when he joined trumpeter June Clark's band. He played baritone saxophone with Earl Hines's band later that year, and then joined Horace Henderson. In the next few years, he worked with many of the top bands of the time, including those of Charlie Johnson, Don Redman, drummers Bill McKinney ("McKinney's Cotton Pickers") and Chick Webb, and, on several different occasions, Fletcher Henderson. He started his career as an arranger with Johnson's band.

Carter formed his own group (which included Teddy Wilson) in 1933, wrote arrangements for Benny Goodman, and briefly joined bands led by reedman Charlie Barnet and vocalist Willie Bryant. In 1935, he went to work in Paris for a band led by reedman Willie Lewis. He liked Europe and stayed abroad until 1938 (serving, among other things, as staff arranger for the BBC house band in London). From 1939 until the mid-1940s, he led big and small ensembles in New York and Hollywood, and in 1945, he moved permanently to the West Coast.

Since taking up residence in California, Carter has continued to make small-band jazz recordings, but he has devoted most of his time to composing and arranging music for films, television (including work for Bob Hope and the Alfred Hitchcock series), and popular singers from Pearl Bailey, Sarah Vaughan, and Ray Charles to Debbie Reynolds and Rod McKuen. He has also done considerable lecturing and performing in collegiate jazz education programs.

Carter has been one of the best and most productive arrangers in jazz history. He was particularly good at writing richly textured reed parts and reed/brass interplays for the bands of the swing era, but he was never a slave to swing and was able for many years to keep his musical ideas fresh and modern. Even today, arrangements of his from the 1930s sound alive and up-to-date.

Carter rarely records on trumpet anymore, but when he did record, he was a modest but highly competent performer, with a smooth, relaxed tone that rarely calls attention to itself. As an alto saxophonist, he was one of the major reed players of the 1930s and early 1940s, and he is nearly always a great pleasure to listen to, with his great technical skill and elegant, effortlessly decorated sound.

Selected Recordings

Benny Carter (Prestige)
Big Band Bounce (Capitol)
Aspects (United Artists)
Swingin' the 20s (Contemporary)
Further Definitions (Impulse)
Carter, Gillespie, Inc. (Pablo)

The Prestige album includes early Carter small-band recordings from around 1939. Half of the Capitol LP is devoted to bands Carter led in New York, Los Angeles, and San Francisco from 1943 to 1945, just before he moved permanently to California. (The other half of the album is by trumpeter Cootie Williams.) *Aspects* is small-group material from the late 1950s. The Contemporary recording matches Carter with pianist Earl Hines and is one of his relatively few quartet dates. The Impulse album, from the early 1960s, is extremely enjoyable, swinging material featuring Coleman Hawkins, Phil Woods, and Basie drummer Jo Jones, and the Pablo LP, dating from 1976, shows Carter in a bop context, along with trumpeter Dizzy Gillespie.

–5–

Bop and Post-Bop

s swing sweetened and jazz in general grew more polished and accomplished, some of the more restlessly imaginative young players of the music started questioning their elders' musical assumptions. Paying close attention to the hints of radical tonal, harmonic, and rhythmic ideas in the work of musicians like Art Tatum, Lester Young, Coleman Hawkins, and Charlie Christian, these younger players broke old rules, invented new ways to sounding on their instruments. They called this new music "bop."

It is impossible to say who the first real bop musician was, but the first true giant of bop, its most fecund, influential, and virtuosic practitioner, was saxophonist Charlie Parker, one of the greatest figures jazz has had in any style or era.

The Musicians

Parker came from Kansas City, where he had achieved some recognition with a band led by Jay McShann, a good blues pianist who led a swing orchestra. In 1939, Parker went to New York, where he spent many hours sitting in on sessions in bars and nightclubs.

In Kansas City, Parker had already developed a unique sound on alto saxophone, built around a precise, neatly rounded, almost brash, shiny tone. In New York, he apparently was able to apply this sound to ideas that had been forming in his head. In a book of jazz musicians' recollections called *Hear Me Talkin' to Ya* (edited by Nat Shapiro and Nat Hentoff), he recalls how, one night in December 1939, he was playing "Cherokee" in a "chili house" in Harlem. Suddenly, it came to him that "by using the higher intervals of a chord as a melody line and backing them with appropriately related [chord] changes I could play the thing I'd been hearing. I came alive."

Fortunately for Parker (and for jazz), when he made his breakthrough, there were people who could understand where he had gone and who knew how to set out on the same path themselves. One of these was a fine young trumpeter named John Birks Gillespie, nicknamed "Dizzy" for his unpredictable personality and his sense of humor. Gillespie was fired from singer Cab Calloway's band in 1941—partly because he developed his own way of phrasing and uncommon harmonic ideas that were similar to Parker's.

Another man whose musical eccentricities got him into trouble with his employer was Kenny Clarke, who might be called the first modern jazz drummer, for the way he changed the basic time-keeping functions of the drum kit to give the drummer more flexibility and rhythmic subtlety and make him an equal partner to the other musicians. Unfortunately, Clarke was working with a conventional swing band led by saxophonist Teddy Hill (who had also once employed Dizzy Gillespie) when he started developing his new theories, and Hill felt, quite correctly, that such novel notions didn't belong on a swing bandstand.

The Clubs

In 1940, Teddy Hill retired from bandleading to become manager of a club in Harlem called Minton's Playhouse. One of his

first acts was to ask the drummer he had once fired, Kenny
Clarke, to organize a house band. Clarke hired Thelonius Monk
for piano, a bass player named Nick Fenton, and a good swing
trumpeter named Joe Guy (who later played prominently on a
number of Billie Holiday records). With this band as the core,
Minton's became a popular site for jam sessions and occasional
informal performances by musicians with various musical styles,
but most of those who played there had leanings toward what
would soon be known as bop.

Minton's, Monroe's, and the clubs along 52nd Street in New
York (the Onyx, the Three Deuces, the Spotlight, the Hickory
House, and Birdland) became the focal points of bop in the
early 1940s.

It is usually agreed that the first bop records were some
made in 1944 by a twelve-piece bop-flavored swing band led by
Coleman Hawkins that featured Gillespie, saxophonists Budd
Johnson and Leo Parker (no relation to Charlie), bassist Oscar
Pettiford, and Max Roach on drums. Charlie Parker made his
first real bop records in 1945, with Gillespie and various combinations of bop and swing players. By that time, bop had become the new force in jazz. Among the most important new
figures drawn to it were pianist Bud Powell—the quintessential
bop keyboard player and a far more adept and influential jazz
pianist than the idiosyncratic Thelonious Monk—Miles Davis,
Howard McGhee, Fats Navarro, and Clifford Brown, and—a
relative latecomer to bop—Charles Mingus.

By 1950, bop was an established, full-fledged musical and
cultural phenomenon, with its own tricks of the trade and even
its own traditions. To the general public, bop was something of
a novelty, characterized by (and this was largely the musicians'
own fault) horn-rimmed glasses, goatees, berets, and "cool" or
"hep" (later "hip") behavior. To musicians, it was a kind of jazz
that sounded different from any jazz preceding it, because it
was built with different tools and materials.

The Musical Structure

In bop, harmonic rules were stretched almost to the breaking
point as more and more notes became "permissible" (often
through half-step chord shifts or implications of chords). More
than one observer has pointed out that bop's biggest innovation
was rhythmic, and not harmonic: rhythmically, bop was looser
and more subtle, more versatile and more complex than earlier
jazz styles. Bop musicians played more notes than their predecessors had, filling space more densely. They started accenting
measures on the second and fourth, instead of the first and
third beats—or accenting them off the beats altogether. They
banished swing inflections.

Bop also created some new jazz traditions—organizational
traditions, they might be called. These included new roles for
the bass and piano: the bass instrument took on some of the
bass drum's old time-keeping function while developing into
more of a melodic voice, and the piano lost some of its rhythmic solidity to create sparer, lighter lines. In addition, there was
a standard quintet format of piano, bass, drums, reed instru-

ment, and trumpet (sometimes augmented by a trombone or a second reed instrument, and occasionally including a guitar in the rhythm section) and a standard structure of a tune—statement of theme, reed solo, trumpet solo, piano solo, bass or drum solo every second or third or fourth number (sometimes there were both a bass solo and a drum solo, often on the closing tune). Sometimes, in a single tune there would be a period of "trading fours"—alternating four-bar improvised passages between instruments (usually, the bass or drums, on one hand, and each solo instrument in its turn, on the other). Generally, each number would be rounded off with a restatement of the original theme.

One other device—which certainly appeared in jazz before bop, but which bop refined and validated—is the frequent insertion of "quotes," brief passages from or references to easily recognizable melodies, into solos based on another melody.

Bop never became a really popular form of music the way swing did. This was partly because much of it wasn't recorded—due to recording bans from 1942 to 1944, and in 1948—but it was mostly the nature of the music itself that kept it from catching fire. Bop did not play to its audiences. To begin with, bop musicians rarely, if ever, thought of their music as entertainment; jazz became "art" for the first time. More importantly, bop didn't offer much in the way of melody, familiar "hooks" for the listener to grab onto, and it was hardly music for people to dance to.

As a pure form, bop didn't last for long after the death of Charlie Parker in 1955, and some distinct variations on it started to appear long before that time. But the bop vocabulary, and, even more so, the bop sensibility, led to almost all of the "modern" jazz of the 1950s and 1960s.

Cool Jazz

One variation of bop was "cool" jazz—which had at least two important and distinctly different manifestations to begin with. One of these was the remarkable ensemble formed by trumpeter Miles Davis for several brief engagements in 1948 (and reformed for some recording sessions in 1949 and 1950). The instrumentation of the group was unique. Besides the conventional piano, bass, and drums, there were trumpet, trombone, French horn, tuba, and alto and baritone saxophones. The music was light and lyrical, and was largely written, not improvised. Davis's group had limited exposure, but it employed some noteworthy talents and its music was widely listened to and taken to heart by other musicians.

Another kind of cool was practiced by pianist Lennie Tristano, who was in many ways the founder of the avant-garde in jazz. The Davis group was cool in the sense that its sound was light and spare and texturally delicate. Tristano and his disciples—the most important of whom were saxophonists Lee Konitz and Warne Marsh and guitarist Billy Bauer—were cool in the emotional and intellectual sense. Their music was carefully charted and precise, and some of the feeling was taken out of it intentionally (for instance, the pianist instructed his bassist and drummer to play without inflections, so that the position of bar lines in the music became vague). Davis and Tristano both influenced other cool jazz musicians. California became a center for this style of music, thanks largely to Gerry Mulligan, who worked with an unusual piano less quartet (at first, with trumpeter Chet Baker and later with valve trombonist Bob Brookemeyer or trumpeter Jon Eardley), and to pianist Dave Brubeck. Brubeck was a student of classical composer Darius Milhaud, and his early records feature elegant little fugues and variations that helped to add a European, academic calm to cool jazz.

Meanwhile, some of the popular and important musicians of the swing era began to accommodate some bop influences and bop musicians, into their work. Very few well-developed swing players were ever able to really play bop or bop-derived jazz. One of the more successful at this was clarinetist/saxophonist Woody Herman, who had led good swing bands through the late 1930s and the 1940s. Perhaps his relative success in bop was due to his most famous band, the 1948 edition. In it, Herman introduced a new reed section so powerful and cohesive that its members were called "The Four Brothers." These four were Stan Getz, Zoot Sims, Serge Chaloff, and Herbie Steward, some of whom gained subsequent recognition as important bop and/or post-bop players.

Perhaps the most important, and certainly the most long-lived, ensemble to present this side of the jazz idiom to the public was the eloquent Modern Jazz Quartet. The group's roots were firmly in bop: it grew out of the rhythm section with Dizzy Gillespie's big band of the late 1940s. This section included pianist John Lewis, bassist Ray Brown, drummer Kenny Clarke, and vibraharpist Milt Jackson. (The "vibes" was perfectly suited for this kind of music, both for its cool sound and for its relative inability to inflect notes.) When the quartet started performing away from the band, under Jackson's leadership, Brown was replaced by Percy Heath. The group first recorded in 1952 and officially became a working band in 1954. When Clarke moved to Paris in 1956, he was replaced by Connie Kay. After that, the group remained intact until 1974, when Jackson resigned.

The MJQ played exacting, almost precious music that referred constantly to jazz (and specifically, even in their last few years, to bop) but was some indefinable combination of jazz, popular, and classical music. Still, they could play hard-swinging, straight jazz when they wanted to, and they doubtless exposed many listeners to it by first winning their good graces with a more delicate brand of music.

Hard Bop

While jazz was being cooled down, Europeanized, repopularized, and, perhaps, attenuated, there was also a movement afoot to re-energize it, to harden it up again, to give it back the soul that some people thought it had lost. New York, the place from which bop emerged, was the center of this movement, sometimes called "hard bop." Its two most important leaders were drummer Art Blakey and a pianist named Horace Silver. Blakey had had some success as a pure bop drummer with Billy Eckstine's big band, among other groups, and Silver first gained recognition in the last days of the original bop movement as a member of Stan Getz's quintet.

Blakey was, and is, a thunderously solid drummer whose most obvious influence was Max Roach. In 1955, Blakey formed a group called The Jazz Messengers, a quintet with Silver, bassist Doug Watkins, tenor saxophonist Hank Mobley, and trumpeter Kenny Dorham. With only brief interruptions, Blakey has led a quintet or sextet under the same name ever since. His groups have included an astonishing number of important musicians, often in their formative years, and he is well-known and respected as a leader who builds other leaders. Among his alumni are Freddie Hubbard, Woody Shaw, Chuck Mangione, Jackie McLean, Wayne Shorter, and Keith Jarrett. Although the character of the Jazz Messengers has changed over the years, it has always been a strong, hard-driving group with impressive solo work and simple but effective ensemble passages.

Funk and Hard Bop

A similarly intense group—although it didn't last as long nor produce so consistently strong a body of solo work—was Horace Silver's quintet. Silver founded his group in 1956. By the end of the 1950s, the band had found its identity as a funky, blues-based, hard-bop quintet that was best known for easily remembered soulful melodies and for Silver's own solos, which were often built around pretty little blues melodies harmonically related to the original melodic line. Like Blakey, Silver employed very good musicians, but he was never as obvious an influence on developing talents as Blakey was.

The other major hard-bop group was that led by alto saxophonist Cannonball Adderly. The Adderly band was always very bright, direct and enjoyable to hear, although never particularly complicated musically. In their prime, they had numerous funky jazz hits, including versions of Timmons's "This Here" and "Dat Dere," Nat Adderly's "Jive Samba" and "Work Song," and Cannonball Adderly's "Sack o' Woe."

More firmly in the soul jazz mold were the piano/bass/drums trios led by pianists Ramsey Lewis in Chicago and Les McCann in Los Angeles; the Hammond organ/guitar/drums trios, sometimes augmented by a saxophone, led by organists Jimmy Smith, Jimmy McGriff, and Richard "Groove" Holmes; a group from Texas called The Jazz Crusaders (which is still in existence as The Crusaders); and the octet, led by singer/pianist/saxophonist Ray Charles, which played superb jazz in and around the rhythm and blues for which its leader was best known.

The main thrust of bop, hard bop, and cool jazz was over by the early 1960s, but elements of these styles have survived into the present. Far more than New Orleans or Chicago jazz styles, or even swing, have done, they have animated and helped to define jazz as most of us know it.

CHARLIE PARKER *(1920–55)*

Much of the best jazz of the 1920s and 1930s was played in Kansas City, and Charles Christopher Parker grew up in the midst of it. He had some limited exposure to music in school, and his mother bought him an alto saxophone when he was 11. (He later said that listening to Rudy Vallee on the radio had first got him interested in that horn.) He seems to have been a slow starter, and there are contemporary stories of Parker being humiliated when he tried to sit in with more accomplished musicians at local jam sessions. He was very serious about his music, however, and practiced long and hard until he improved.

In 1937, Parker went to work for Buster Smith, the musician he admired most. Smith was a good clarinetist and an alto saxophonist with a warm, confident tone, who had played with Walter Page's Blue Devils, had taken over leadership of the group when Page left, and now was forming his own twelve-piece group. Parker stayed with the band for several months; then he joined a small group led by pianist Jay McShann.

Parker had by this time developed into a strong, unique soloist, and was a great musical inspiration to the rest of the band—so much so that McShann made him the deputy leader of the group. However, Parker had been introduced to heroin when he was about 15, and it was beginning to become a serious problem, causing him to miss work or fall asleep on the bandstand. Parker took a leave from the McShann band and went to New York in 1939. There, he had his harmonic breakthrough playing "Cherokee", and there he was first heard by Dizzy Gillespie, Kenny Clarke, and other founders of bop. He returned to McShann, and, in 1942, played the Savoy Ballroom in New York with the band. He left New York with McShann but soon turned back, this time for good.

Parker played at Minton's Playhouse and other such clubs, listened, and traded ideas. For money, he took a nine-month engagement with vocalist Noble Sissle's definitely non-jazz orchestra, playing clarinet as well as alto saxophone. In 1943, he joined Earl Hines's band, playing tenor saxophone. When Billy Eckstine formed his bop-era big band, featuring some of Parker's cohorts from Minton's, Parker joined for a short time. In 1945, Parker and Gillespie made their first recordings together, under Gillespie's name, with two different transitional swing/bop rhythm sections. This was still not full-blown bop, but Parker and Gillespie were already well-defined soloists.

In late November 1945, Parker made his first recordings under his own leadership, with Gillespie and Miles Davis on trumpet, Argonne Thornton (later known as Sadik Hakim) on piano, Curley Russell on bass, and Max Roach on drums. Parker made some middling quartet and septet recordings in 1946 and then, mid-year, suffered a full-scale breakdown and was committed to Camarillo State Hospital.

He was released six months later and began a period of intense recording activity and creative growth. Many of the definitive Parker performances, with Miles Davis, J. J. Johnson, John Lewis, Hank Jones, and Duke Jordan, among others, date from 1947 and 1948. Parker worked with Jazz at the Philharmonic, toured Europe, made his fine recordings with strings and some occasionally successful ones with Afro-Cuban players.

After Camarillo, Parker was intermittently free from heroin addiction, but he started drinking heavily to compensate and soon developed stomach ulcers and liver problems. In the early 1950s, both his playing and his behavior were erratic. In 1952, he made some strong recordings with a big band, and the next year, he recorded the famous "Jazz at Massey Hall" concert in Toronto, with Gillespie, Bud Powell, Charles Mingus, and Max Roach. His last really good recordings were two quartet dates in 1952 and 1953, one with Al Haig on piano, the other with Hank Jones.

Parker's young daughter Pree died of pneumonia the next year, and he never really recovered from the blow. He drank iodine in a suicide attempt and spent time in Bellevue. He recorded again, with pianist Walter Bishop and guitarist Billy Bauer, but his playing sounded embarassingly gruff and wavering. In 1955 he was booked into Birdland—perhaps the most famous of the 52nd Street jazz clubs—with Kenny Dorham, Bud Powell, Charles Mingus, and Art Blakey. His opening night was a fiasco, including an argument with Powell on the bandstand. Mingus took over the microphone to denounce the "sickness" of the whole episode, and Parker stalked out. On March 12, he died in a friend's apartment while watching Jimmy Dorsey on television. Trouble had so aged him that although he was only 35, the death certificate gave his age as 55.

Parker's influence on the course of jazz—and much of popular music—is almost impossible to overestimate. He influenced jazz players of every kind, invented a new kind of music, and was a formidable performer

Selected Recordings

Jay McShann and His Orchestra (Coral)
Dizzy Gillespie: In the Beginning (two-record set, Prestige)
Bird/The Savoy Recordings (Master Takes) (Savoy)
The Very Best of Bird (two-record set, Warners)
Bird at the Roost (Savoy)
The Verve Years (1948–50) (two-record set, Verve)
The Greatest Jazz Concert Ever (Prestige)

Parker is identifiable on the McShann recordings, especially on

"Hootie Blues." The Gillespie album is composed of original Parker/Gillespie 1945 recordings. The Savoy reissue includes both Parker's first small-group recordings and the first recordings released under his own name. It then proceeds through four top-notch Parker quintets from 1947 and 1948. The Warners LP has some of Parker's best material, originally recorded in 1946 and 1947. The other Savoy recording is a series of radio broadcasts from 1949 featuring Kenny Dorham, Al Haig, Tommy Potter, Max Roach, and, on some tracks, Lucky Thompson and Milt Jackson. The recording quality is muddy, and some of the playing has a desultory air about it, but there's plenty of good, intense music, too. The Verve set includes some recordings with strings, some strong quintet work (with Gillespie, Roach, Monk, Dorham, Haig, and others) from 1949–50, and a quartet date with Hank Jones.The Prestige set includes the splendid Jazz at Massey Hall concert by Parker and the rhythm section of Powell, Mingus, and Roach.

DIZZY GILLESPIE   *(John Birks Gillespie) (1917–   )*

When he was a boy in a town called Cheraw, South Carolina, Dizzy Gillespie was consistently exposed to music: his father was an amateur musician and played in a band whose instruments resided with the Gillespies between sessions, so Dizzy Gillespie tried them out. When he was 14, he started concentrating on trombone at school, and some months after that, he picked up his first trumpet. He won a scholarship to study music theory at Laurinburg Institute in North Carolina, and when his family moved to Philadelphia in 1935, he had learned enough to play his first jobs.

In Philadelphia Gillespie worked in one trumpet section with his contemporary Charlie Shavers (best known as the composer of "Undecided"), whose flashy swing style and musical sense of humor later influenced his work. A much more important influence on Gillespie, though, was the definitive swing trumpeter Roy Eldridge, whose work he heard in Philadelphia and whose sound and sense he copied closely for some years.

Gillespie left Philadelphia to take a job in New York, but it fell through, and in 1937, he was hired instead by Teddy Hill (later the manager of Minton's Playhouse) to take the place vacated by Roy Eldridge. That year, Gillespie recorded his first solos with the band, sounding very much indeed like a younger version of his idol. It is said that he even had other musicians transcribe Eldridge solos for him so that he could play them note for note.

Gillespie toured Europe with Hill, then freelanced in New York, and in 1939, joined Cab Calloway. His style began to evolve, as did his new ideas about harmonic improvisation. While working with Calloway, and then with various other swing bands, he played at Minton's Playhouse and elsewhere after hours, working with Charlie Parker, Charlie Christian, Thelonious Monk, Kenny Clarke, and others to create what became known as bop.

In 1943, at the Onyx on 52nd Street, he co-led with bassist Oscar Pettiford a small band including Max Roach, tenor saxophonist Don Byas, and pianist George Wallington. Billy Eckstine was alternating sets with the group at the Onyx when he decided to form his own big band, which Gillespie and Parker and other fledgling bop players joined. In 1945, Gillespie recorded under his own name for the first time—initially, with a sextet including tenor saxophonist Dexter Gordon and drummer Shelley Manne, and then with Charlie Parker. That year, he also formed his first big band. Despite good arrangements by Walter Fuller and good solo work by Gillespie and fellow trumpeter Kenny Dorham, it was less than successful. Throughout the rest of the 1940s, he toured and recorded with various groups, including several excellent big bands.

Despite the identification of Gillespie with Charlie Parker, the two worked together comparatively little in the 1940s. They did rejoin forces in 1950, along with Thelonious Monk, to make an excellent album for Norman Granz's Verve label and were again reunited in 1953 for the "Jazz at Massey Hall" concert in Toronto. In the early 1950s, Gillespie worked frequently with Afro-Cuban percussionists and with bop singers like Kenny Hagood and Joe Carroll. He also sang bop songs himself and continued to inject comedy into his music.

In 1951, he started his own record label, Dee Gee, and two years later he began a long association with Verve. In 1956, he formed another big band—this time under the auspices of the U.S. State Department—which undertook two world tours. In 1958, he formed a quintet again, and he continued to work in that context, off and on, until 1971, when the group became a quartet. Saxophonists Leo Wright and James Moody and pianists Junior Mance, Kenny Barron, and Lalo Schifrin were among the musicians that Gillespie employed. He did film soundtracks and appeared in concert settings, performing works written especially for him, and he has reformed his big band on several occasions. Gillespie is still active.

Gillespie was the co-founder of modern jazz, an immensely intelligent musician who seemed to think up new challenges for himself and other musicians almost as fast as he met the old ones. As a soloist, he was the most distinctive trumpet voice around for more than a decade, and he remained a strong, inventive player for at least a decade more. He has a bright, brassy sound that bristles with excitement and a wondrous firmness of tone. Even his humor, for which he has sometimes been maligned, has added a refreshing quality to what sometimes threatens to become ponderously serious music. As a composer, he has provided the world with such bop standards as "A Night in Tunisia," "Con Alma," "Woody'n You," "Groovin' High," "Manteca," "Anthropology," and "Blue 'n' Boogie"—all of them jewels in the jazz canon. As a cultural force, leading bands of fine musicians all over the world, he has helped to give native American music a name.

Selected Recordings

In the Beginning (two-record set, Prestige)
The Dizzy Gillespie Orchestra at Salle Pleyel (Prestige)
Dee Gee Days (two-record set, Savoy)
Dizzy, Rollins & Stitt (Verve)
Dizzy Meets Sonny (Verve)
Diz and Getz (Verve)
An Electrifying Evening with the Dizzy Gillespie Quintet (Verve)
Dizzy on the French Riviera (Philips)

The first Prestige album offers the 1945 sextet work with Dexter Gordon and Shelly Manne, the famous Charlie Parker/Clyde Hart and Charlie Parker/Al Haig dates from the same year, a 1946 sextet recording with Sonny Stitt and Milt Jackson, a number of 1946 big-band recordings, and a seldom-heard sextet date from 1950, with Jimmy Heath and Jackson—a good mix of Gillespie at his early prime. The Salle Pleyel album, recorded in Paris in 1948, is powerful big-band stuff. The Savoy album includes all the tracks that Gillespie recorded for his own label in 1951 and 1952. Of particular interest is the presence of young John Coltrane playing alto and tenor saxophones on a few tracks; the performances by tenor saxophonist Budd Johnson and violinist Stuff Smith, and by Milt Jackson, playing piano and singing; and the inclusion of early appearances by pianist Wynton Kelly and guitarist Kenny Burrell. There is also plenty of clowning and plenty of scat singing by Gillespie, Joe Carroll, Melvin Moore, and others.

The first Verve album is a classic, with two superb tenor saxophonists, Sonny Rollins and Sonny Stitt, playing at top form and Gillespie himself sounding absolutely confident and supremely imaginative. (There are four long tracks here, one each with Rollins and Stitt, and two with both of them.) Stitt is heard again with Gillespie on the second Verve LP, which features John Lewis on piano and Skeeter Best on guitar and contains a beautiful ballad medley on which Gillespie adequately proves that he has a lyrical, subtle side. The Getz tracks, from 1953 and 1956, also feature Stitt somewhat, although he plays alto saxophone here, and not the tenor for which he is best known. Max Roach plays very well on some of the 1953 tracks on which Stitt doesn't appear, and Getz sounds surprisingly hearty at times. The last Verve recording is typical, strong early 1960s quintet material featuring a famous Gillespie tour de force called "Kush." The Philips album offers a beautiful version of "No More Blues," and a work by Gypsy violinist Elek Baesik.

THELONIOUS MONK   *(1920–   )*

Born in North Carolina and brought up in New York City, Thelonious Monk seems to have become interested in the piano at an early age. He may have taken some lessons as a child, although his technical limitations and highly idiosyncratic style suggest that he was largely self-taught. Little is known of his early years as a musician (except that he toured with an evangelist for a period) until he turned up around Minton's and such places in the late 1930s. He quickly became an associate of musicians like Kenny Clarke, Dizzy Gillespie, and Charlie Parker, and his music followed a strongly individualistic musical direction in the early days of the formation of bop.

Monk was in the house band that Kenny Clarke formed at Minton's in 1940; joined vocalist Lucky Millinder's band in 1942; worked briefly with Coleman Hawkins in 1944, and off and on with Dizzy Gillespie in the later 1940s; and in 1950, he recorded with Gillespie and Charlie Parker. For most of his career, however, he has worked with his own groups, including everything from trios to 10-piece bands, and all of them shaped closely to his own musical ideas.

Monk's first recordings as a leader were made for Blue Note in 1947, but it was his work for Prestige in the early 1950s and Riverside in the late 1950s that gained him his reputation, while the albums that he made for Columbia in the 1960s kept it alive. His repertoire includes a few standards ("These Foolish Things," "Smoke Gets in Your Eyes," for example), but the greater part of it consists of a small group of his own compositions (some of them based on the chord changes of standards). The most famous of these are " 'Round Midnight" (itself something of a standard), "Well, You Needn't," "Straight, No Chaser," "In Walked Bud," "Evidence," "Ruby, My Dear," "Little Rootie Tootie," and his perennial closing theme, "Epistrophy." An impressive roster of musicians has worked with him through the years, including three of the greatest saxophonists jazz has had: Coleman Hawkins, John Coltrane, and Sonny Rollins. He has also worked with Gerry Mulligan, and Max Roach and Art Blakey. Perhaps his best-known groups, though, were two one-time-only big bands that he assembled for New York concerts in 1959 and 1963—both played arrangements by composer/pianist Hall Overton and both featured assemblages of excellent musicians—and his quartet of the early 1960's with tenor saxophonist Charlie Rouse. He has also made several recordings of solo piano on which his stride roots become even more apparent than usual.

As both pianist and composer, Monk is so unusual, with his slow, thoughtful, ragged, understated manner and his almost subversive harmonic sense, that it is hard to say exactly what were his musical roots: Art Tatum was certainly important to him, and there are bits of Earl Hines and even Duke Ellington in his playing, but the total effect is uniquely his.

It is even harder to say just what other pianists he influenced. There are hints of Monk in the work of such fine post-bop players as Randy Weston, Jaki Byard, and Mal Waldron, to be sure. There are also clear echoes of Monk's ideas in some of the work of his great champion Bud Powell (sometimes in the form of the vaguely lagging, almost dissonant glissandos that Monk is so fond of playing). However, if others have influenced Monk or been influenced by him, Monk himself is one of a kind, a true original who shines brightly as one of the true stars of jazz.

Selected Recordings

Genius of Modern Music (two volumes) (Blue Note)
Monk (two-record reissue) (Prestige)
Pure Monk (two-record reissue) (Milestone)
Monk/Trane (two-record reissue) (Milestone)
Thelonious Monk In Person (two-record reissue) (Milestone)
Monk Big Band and Quartet in Concert (Columbia)

The original Blue Note LPs offer Monk in various trio, quartet, and quintet contexts—often with Milt Jackson and always with Art Blakey. Early versions of many of his most famous compositions ("Straight, No Chaser" and "Ruby, My Dear," for example) are included. A wealth of fine Monk recordings is available in recent reissue: the Prestige material, from 1952 through 1954, includes some of Monk's best trio work, as well as one quintet with Sonny Rollins and French horn player Julius Watkins and another with Ray Copeland and Frank Foster. *Pure Monk* is Riverside material, including nothing but solo piano, that was culled from six different albums and features a substantial representation of standards. The second Milestone reissue, also originally from Riverside, includes most of the classic *Thelonious Monk and John Coltrane* LP that was issued in 1958 on Jazzland (a Riverside label) and most of the truly wonderful *Monk's Music* album from 1957. The latter featured Coltrane, Coleman Hawkins, Gigi Gryce, Ray Copeland, Art Blakey, and bassist Wilbur Ware.

The in-person set is two complete Riverside LPs—one devoted to the 1959 big-band concert at New York's Town Hall, and the other to a session at San Francisco's Blackhawk Club at which Monk's quartet with Charlie Rouse was augmented by the fine West Coast tenor player Harold Land and by trumpeter Joe Gordon. The Columbia recording, as its title indicates, offers both Monk's quartet (with Rouse) and a large band in concert—this time in 1963 at New York's Philharmonic Hall. There are numerous later Columbia LPs with the Rouse quar-

tet and with Monk solo, but they contain very little that the regular listener to Monk will not have heard by this time.

BUD POWELL   *(Earl Powell) (1924–66)*

Bud Powell was born in New York City into a family of amateur and professional musicians. He began his music studies, both formal and informal, at an early age, and by the age of 10, his father later remembered, "He could play everything he'd heard by Fats Waller and Art Tatum." He left school as a teenager and found jobs as a pianist in Coney Island clubs and in variety shows of various kinds. At some point, he met Thelonious Monk, who introduced him to the Minton's scene. He quickly came under the influence of Charlie Parker and Charlie Christian and was soon working out his own versions of their ideas on piano.

Powell's first important professional engagement was with trumpeter Cootie Williams's band in 1943 and 1944, and it was with this group that he made his first recordings. He became a fixture of the 52nd Street scene, playing with a seemingly endless succession of small groups throughout the late 1940s and early 1950s, with saxophonists Sonny Stitt, Dexter Gordon, and Don Byas, trombonist J. J. Johnson, trumpeter Fats Navarro, and others. He also recorded a substantial amount of solo piano and trio work during this period—mostly for Verve and Blue Note—which remains his strongest playing on records. Ironically, although Powell is nearly always mentioned with Charlie Parker and Dizzy Gillespie as a founder of bop, he played with these two men relatively seldom, and recorded with them even less often.

From his late teens, Powell had trouble with narcotics and alcohol, and he suffered from various mental and physical disorders most of his life. He served his first term in a mental institution when he was 21 and was in and out of hospitals and sanitoriums all his life. In the mid- to late 1950s, he was in institutions most of the time, although he continued to play regularly around the New York area whenever he was at liberty.

In 1959, his health greatly improved, Powell moved to Paris, where he formed a trio with French bassist Pierre Michelot and Kenny Clarke, the founder of bop drumming (who had moved there in 1956). He was active in Paris for several years, playing frequently at Left Bank clubs and recording with his old compatriots Don Byas (who had gone to Europe on tour with saxophonist Don Redman's band in 1946 and decided not to return to America) and Dexter Gordon (who spent the early 1960s in Copenhagen and Paris). Despite his success, he continued to drink heavily, and in 1962, he contracted tuberculosis.

In 1964, after a period of recuperation in France, Powell returned to the United States on what was supposed to be a short visit to play an engagement at Birdland. When the job was finished, however, he refused to go back to France. When he died in Brooklyn in 1966 of tuberculosis, alcoholism, and malnutrition, he had been almost completely inactive for two years.

Powell was an astonishing pianist. He was technically accomplished and possessed an almost encyclopedic knowledge of earlier jazz piano styles, which he could incorporate happily into his own playing. At the same time, his playing was completely original: he practically defined bop and post-bop piano playing, as surely as Charlie Parker defined that music on his own instrument. Powell's harmonic sense and physical style—the spare left hand, the right hand undertaking journeys whose speed and scope was practically unprecedented on piano, the vivid dynamic sense—have spread into almost every corner of the jazz of the past thirty years and have been built upon frequently (and occasionally very well). He must be counted as one of the major architects of jazz.

Selected Recordings

Bud Powell Vol. 1 (Blue Note)
Bud Powell Vol. 2 (Blue Note)
Time Waits (Blue Note)
The Scene Changes (Blue Note)
The Genius of Bud Powell (two-record set, Verve)
Bud Powell in Paris (Reprise)
Our Man in Paris by Dexter Gordon (Blue Note)

The Blue Note albums and the Verve two-record re-issue, all dating from 1949 to 1951, are undoubtedly the best Bud Powell on record. Both in solos and with various bassists and drummers (including Ray Brown and Max Roach on some of the Verve sides and Paul Chambers and Art Taylor on some of the Blue Notes), Powell plays a wide assortment of standards and bop tunes, including many of his own compositions. Among these, perhaps most notably, is the wonderful "Tempus Fugit," also known as "Tempus Fugue-it," on the Verve set. His playing is consistently strong and thoughtful on these albums: all his virtues are apparent. The Reprise album features a trio including French bassist Gilbert Rovère and expatriate American drummer Kansas Fields (neither of whom was an exciting musician). It also is rather inconsistent, but Powell sounds strong and, at least occasionally, inventive. The Dexter Gordon recording, with Pierre Michelot and Kenny Clarke, shows Powell off to better advantage: his playing here is strong (though not as well modulated as it once was), rather bluesy, and lean. This latter quality may well be the result of physical limitations that had visited Powell by this time, but it is effective, by and large.

CHARLES MINGUS   *(1922–79)*

Born in Nogales, Arizona, and brought up in Los Angeles, Charles Mingus started studying music formally at the age of 8— first on trombone, and later on cello. He switched to bass to play in his high school dance band and studied that instrument with the noted bassist/tuba player Red Callender. Callender had been working with Louis Armstrong, and Mingus himself joined Armstrong in 1941, remaining with the trumpeter for two years. He subsequently joined a New Orleans revival group with jazz pioneers Barney Bigard and Kid Ory and played with guitarist Alvino Rey's band, which was largely dedicated to "sweet" sounds and musical novelties.

Throughout this period, Mingus continued his musical studies—primarily with a former bassist with the New York Philharmonic Orchestra—and by late 1946, when he joined Lionel Hampton's band, he had become an extraordinarily good musician. In 1947, he made his recording debut, with Hampton, playing a composition of his own called "Mingus Fingers." In 1950, he joined an innovative chamber-jazz trio led by vibraharpist Red Norvo (with guitarist Tal Farlow). He left the group in 1951 and moved to New York, where he joined a trio led by pianist Billy Taylor and became a regular on 52nd Street.

By the mid-1950s, Mingus's reputation had grown on many fronts: as a bassist with remarkable technical skills (his only real rival in this regard was Oscar Pettiford); as an extremely powerful and imaginative composer; and as a demanding but inspiring leader of other musicians.

His first groups of the mid- and late-1950s had references to the concert jazz idiom and to conventional European composition. Many of his early collaborations as a leader were with musicians associated with those traditions. From the beginning, his music was extremely emotional and sensuous, frequently betraying a much closer identification with raw blues and gospel music than most serious jazz musicians would have dared reveal. From the mid-1950s to the mid-1960s, and again from the early 1970s almost until his death, Mingus led a succession of dazzling groups of all sizes.

Mingus was a fast, clear, and big-toned bassist with seemingly indefatigable energy. As a composer, Mingus was highly imaginative, capable of fusing many musical and emotional elements into an impressive whole. His music could be angry, political, humorous, or tragic, among other things, but it was always honest, strong, and, in its own way, extremely warm. As a leader, Mingus had little use for musicians who didn't come up to his standards. His personnel rosters are remarkable: some of the musicians he hired went on to become major jazz stars (reed player Eric Dolphy, trumpeter Don Ellis); others have remained undeservedly obscure (saxophonist Shafi Hadi, trumpeters Clarence Shaw and Eddie Preston); but the vast majority are men who have become "musicians' musicians". That the music Mingus produced is almost uniformly strong and exciting is due to them almost as much as it is to the amazing musical imagination of the bassist himself.

Selected Recordings

The Red Norvo Trio/The Savoy Sessions (Savoy)
Better Get It in Your Soul (Columbia)
Charles Mingus Presents the Charles Mingus Quartet Featuring Eric Dolphy (Barnaby)
Tia Juana Moods (RCA)
Town Hall Concert (Solid State)
Mingus Plays Piano (Impulse)
Reincarnation of a Lovebird (two-record set, Prestige)
Charles Mingus and Friends in Concert (two-record set, Columbia)
Mingus Moves (Atlantic)

The Norvo LP, with Mingus and Tal Farlow, is topnotch early work by the bassist. The Columbia set is a two-record reissue consisting of two complete albums, both remarkable, called *Mingus Ah Um* (1959) and *Mingus Dynasty* (1960). Many sides of Mingus are displayed here: classical-oriented ("Diane," "Far Wells, Mill Valley"); political ("Fables of Faubus"); soulful (the title song, "Boogie Stop Shuffle"); Ellingtonian, ("Mood Indigo," "Things Ain't What They Used to Be"). These are by eight- and ten-piece bands (with Handy, Ervin, Parlan, Ellis, and Hanna, among others) and neatly define Mingus's compositions for medium-big bands. The first Barnaby LP is an eloquent, exciting quartet date with Dolphy, Curson, and Dannie Richmond that was originally issued on the Candid label. The RCA recording is one of Mingus's most famous—a neat, programmatic album with plenty of strong solos by Knepper, Hadi, and Shaw. The Town Hall album is a remarkable big-band date, recorded live in 1962, featuring Dolphy, Richmond, and McPherson, among other Mingus regulars, as well as such musicians as saxophonists Charlie Mariano, Jerome Richardson, and Pepper Adams, trombonist Quentin Jackson, and trumpeter Clark Terry. The Impulse recording, subtitled "Spontaneous Compositions and Improvisations," displays Mingus's talent as a careful, rich-toned pianist. The Prestige set includes two complete LPs recorded in France in 1970 that were previously available only on the French-based American label. The group here is an excellent sextet (Preston, McPherson, Jones, Byard, and Richmond), and if Mingus himself sounds a little restrained, the others more than make up for it. Included is an especially stirring sixteen-and-a-half-minute version of the bassist's classic "Pithecanthropus Erectus." The Columbia concert album is a two-record set from Mingus's "comeback" appearance at New York's Philharmonic Hall in 1972. Some old Mingus hands are present— Dizzy Gillespie also may be heard on one track as a scat singer. It is all big-band stuff and is remarkably impressive, considering the rather rag-tag nature of the group. The Atlantic LP is one of Mingus's last, from 1974. The group is a quintet, with Richmond, trumpeter Ronald Hampton, reed player George Adams, and pianist Don Pullen. Only Pullen and Richmond sound really comfortable, and Mingus sounds tired, but there are some inspired Mingus compositions here.

LENNIE TRISTANO   *(1919–77)*

Blind since childhood, Chicago-born Lennie Tristano is said to have taught himself to play the piano before he was 7—at which point he began formal instruction on the instrument. He got his first professional job when he was 12, and throughout his teens, while attending the American Conservatory of Music, he worked as pianist and saxophonist/clarinetist in a variety of dance bands and nightclubs. In his early twenties, he taught music at the Christiansen School of Popular Music, and in 1946, he moved to New York to continue his teaching career. He had been drawn to jazz at an early age and had become particularly fond of the music of Art Tatum and Earl Hines. Once in New York, he started hanging around 52nd Street and developing his own framework for musical experimentation. He was perhaps the best-trained jazz musician (in the formal sense) in the area at the time: he was certainly one of those most oriented to "classical" music (during one engagement on 52nd Street, he began each set with an improvisation on Bach).

Tristano drew a small circle of musicians around him—principally, saxophonists Lee Konitz and Warne Marsh and guitarist Billy Bauer—and infused them with his ideas. In 1949, as part of a session for Capitol, Tristano and these three musicians—plus a bassist and a drummer—recorded two atonal, completely improvised tracks called "Intuition" and "Digression". These are usually considered the first recorded examples of what came to be known as "free jazz."

Technically, Tristano was one of the piano virtuosos of jazz: he was so fast and intricate a player that it was deemed necessary on one of his albums to include the disclaimer, "No use is made of multi-tracking, overdubbing, or tape-speeding on any selection." He was perhaps the first avant-garde musician in jazz, anticipating many facets of the new music of the 1960s and 1970s, rhythmically and harmonically. If he is less well-known than he ought to be in this regard, it is probably due largely to the fact that he never won a large public for his music, even in comparative jazz terms. Nevertheless, he did influence other musicians, and his music remains one of the most remarkable aspects of contemporary jazz.

Selected Recordings

Crosscurrents (Capitol)
Lennie Tristano (Atlantic)
The New Tristano (Atlantic)
Descent into the Maelstrom (Inner City)

One side of the Capitol LP is devoted to Tristano's 1949 sextet with Konitz, Marsh, and Bauer. It includes not only "Intuition" and "Digression," but also "Wow" and "Crosscurrents," two of the pianist's most famous compositions, which are, in their own way, almost as unorthodox as the atonal tracks. The other side of the album is devoted to a philosophically related session by clarinetist Buddy De Franco. The first Atlantic recording includes two trio tracks, and is otherwise devoted to a quartet with Konitz, bassist Gene Ramey, and drummer Art Taylor. A number of standards ("You Go to My Head," "All the Things You Are," and "These Foolish Things," to name a few) are included and are completely transformed. The second Atlantic LP is brilliant, fast, complex solo piano. The Inner City album includes both solo and trio work, including the title piece, an "improvised conception from the Edgar Allen Poe story," and some rare later work from as late as 1966.

SONNY ROLLINS   *(Theodore Walter Rollins) (1929–   )*

Sonny Rollins was born in New York City and was exposed to music as a child, but he didn't take up playing seriously until he was in high school and fell under the influence of singer/alto saxophonist Louis Jordan. Rollins learned how to play alto first and then, upon being exposed to the playing of Coleman Hawkins, he switched to tenor. He happened to live near Bud Powell and Thelonious Monk, and he started hanging around the fledgling bop scene. He developed a forceful, tenacious sound on tenor and was soon sitting in successfully with older bop musicians.

Rollins made his first record in 1948, with singer Babs Gonzales, and in the next few years, he worked with Art Blakey, Tadd Dameron, Bud Powell, and especially Miles Davis: one of his more notable appearances was on Davis's classic 1953 sextet date with another tenor saxophonist named "Charlie Chan"—Charlie Parker, using a pseudonym for contractual reasons. In 1956, Rollins joined a famous quintet co-led by Max Roach and Clifford Brown. In 1957, he left Roach and Brown to form his own group—a pianoless trio, which was quite a daring notion at the time.

In 1960, Rollins retired from public musical life. There was some mystery about his motives, and even his whereabouts, for a time: it turned out that he had simply wanted to take a break from his schedule to practice and to make some basic decisions about what directions to pursue in both his playing and his life. In 1961, a writer named Ralph Berton published a short story in the jazz and pop culture magazine *Metronome* about a jazz fan who accidentally encountered a lone saxophonist, playing sublimely, on the Brooklyn Bridge one night. It was a true story, although the bridge had been changed: Rollins had taken to practicing alone on the Williamsburg Bridge at night, both for privacy and to give his neighbors a rest. When he returned to public life in 1961, it was with a quartet featuring guitarist Jim Hall. His first LP since his reappearance, issued in 1962, was called *The Bridge*.

In 1963, Rollins worked with avant-garde trumpeter Don Cherry, who had come to prominence as Ornette Coleman's associate and musical alter ego, and seemed to be reaching towards "free" playing himself. He later retracted somewhat, to a more traditional hard-bop style, although it had a sharp, occasionally jarring edge to it. During this same period, he worked briefly with a quartet featuring ace trumpeter, Freddie Hubbard, and then, in 1966, he began using a pianist again (Ray Bryant at first) in his group.

In the late 1960s and early 1970s, Rollins again retired from public life. Since mid-1971, he has been active again, working numerous club dates in the United States and undertaking an ambitious schedule of European and Asian tours. In the past few years, he has played in an overtly commercial format with strong jazz-rock fusion influences and even attempts at disco.

Rollins had been a successful jazz composer: he is known for such jazz classics as "Oleo," "Airegin," and "St. Thomas," and he also wrote the popular hit "Alfie," from the British motion picture of the same name. However, he has made his greatest contributions to jazz by far as a saxophonist. One of his later compositions is called "The Cutting Edge," and that phrase seems to describe his playing well—not because it breaks new ground, but in the sense that it is hard, crisp, strong, and absolutely decisive. His tone on tenor saxophone is probably the finest, most consistent there is today, and his ideas, regardless of who or what is his back-up, are bright and many-faceted. He has influenced a host of other saxophonists but has always managed, by sheer force of imagination, to remain substantially better than those who follow him.

Selected Recordings

Collectors' Items by Miles Davis (Prestige)
Rollins (two-record set, Prestige)
Saxophone Colossus and More (two-record set, Prestige)
Way Out West (Contemporary)
The Bridge (RCA)
The Cutting Edge (Milestone)

The Miles Davis LP includes the "Charlie Chan" sextet sides and three quintet tracks recorded in 1956. The first Prestige re-issue is an invaluable sampler, including quartet tracks from 1951 with Art Blakey; a 1953 recording with the Modern Jazz Quintet; some sides made in 1954 with Thelonious Monk and the underrated pianist Elmo Hope; a 1955 track with Max Roach and Ray Bryant; two tracks with the famous Max Roach/Clifford Brown quintet (featuring Richie Powell, Bud's brother, on piano); one track with the great Miles Davis quintet of the 1950s—John Coltrane, Red Garland on piano, Paul Chambers on bass, and Philly Joe Jones on drums; and two tracks from Rollins's own highly acclaimed *Saxophone Colossus* album, all from 1956. The second Prestige two-record set also has the entire *Saxophone Colossus,* as well as selections from three other Rollins albums from the same year. The *Colossus* material is particularly good, with Tommy Flanagan on piano, Doug Watkins on bass, and Max Roach on drums. The versions of "St. Thomas" (based on a calypso melody) and "Moritat" are definitive. Among the other material is more from the Roach/Brown group. The Contemporary album is full of humor and is wonderfully rich with good playing. On it, Rollins essays "Western" songs, with bassist Ray Brown and drummer Shelley Manne as sidekicks, and produces extraordinary music against all odds. The RCA album, as mentioned before, features Jim Hall and is Rollins's first recording after his first self-imposed hiatus between jobs. The Milestone album, recorded live at the 1974 Montreux Jazz Festival, is exceptionally vivid, relatively recent Rollins, with a topnotch group including pianist Stanley Cowell, Japanese guitarist Yoshiaki Masuo, and, on one track, the only jazz bagpipe player (also a solid saxophonist), Rufus Harley.

-6-
The Jazz Singers

The first singers in jazz were not really jazz singers: they were pop singers who sang the blues—sometimes accompanied by jazz musicians (who might or might not have been playing jazz) and sometimes not. They were almost entirely female, and although they used traditional blues forms and even traditional blues songs, they had relatively little in common with the great male blues singers like Robert Johnson, Cripple Clarence Lofton, or Big Bill Broonzy.

These singers were working in a new idiom—a kind of refined, mannered blues that flirted with some of the conventions of popular music, neglecting some of the roughness and almost obsessive simplicity of earlier blues forms yet retaining their eerie emotional power.

The first of the singers who was really important to jazz was Ma Rainey, a warm-voiced, Georgia-born singer who maintained close ties to simpler blues idioms; the greatest of them was Rainey's protégé, Bessie Smith. Some others were Ida Cox, Alberta Hunter, Sippie Wallace, Ivie Anderson, Victoria Spivey, Mildred Bailey, and Ethel Waters.

Nearly all of these women grew up contemporaneously with jazz itself. They were clearly drawn to it and influenced by it, and elements of the new jazz sensibility (such as rhythmic subtleties unknown to blues and new ways of phrasing) appeared increasingly in their work. They became jazz singers—although, by nearly anyone's standards, what they were singing was still the blues.

Jazz Singing and Jazz Playing

This brings up an important point: jazz singing doesn't bear the same relationship to other kinds of singing that jazz playing bears to other kinds of instrumental music. The problem in writing about jazz singers is not, as one writer has suggested, that there are so few of them. In fact, there are a lot of them, representing virtually every jazz style and period. The problem is that jazz singing has to be defined differently from jazz playing.

Some have argued that the only true jazz singers are those relatively few bop and avant-garde vocalists who use their voices like other solo jazz instruments—stating a theme (with or without words) and then building an improvisation (almost always wordless) upon that theme, exactly as a saxophonist or pianist would do. This is patent nonsense. Such a definition would exclude Bessie Smith and other early singers, as well as such later, unquestionably great jazz singers as Billie Holiday, Ella Fitzgerald, Lee Wiley, and Sarah Vaughan.

The point is that the human voice in jazz (or in any other kind of music) simply doesn't have the flexibility that other instruments do. This is not a question of vocal range, but rather of what might be called psychological limitations. The human voice is the instrument most familiar to us, most laden with associative emotional baggage: thus we don't permit it very many unexpected tricks. Non-verbal singing can go only so far before it starts to sound wrong to us, no matter how musically "right" it might be. Lots of Charlie Parker fans thought (and still think) that bop vocalists like Babs Gonzales or Leo Watson were just plain silly. Audiences who listened attentively to avant-garde saxophonist Archie Shepp did an aural double-take when they first heard singer Leone Thomas essay his Central-African–derived jazz yodeling. Singing with words is even more restricted.

In a good song, words and music are inextricably linked—ideally, in a way that makes them greater than the sum of their parts. Tampering with either words or music, then, is a dangerous business: it can be done a little bit, but it cannot be carried too far.

The jazz singer is thus tied more firmly to his or her source material, to the original song or theme, than the jazz instrumentalist is—and as a result, jazz singing has had to develop its own rules, its own premises of improvisation: in short, its own notion of "jazzness."

What jazz singing has developed is a manner of addressing music in which jazz sense, jazz posture, is the operative concept. Instead of improvising on a theme or a line of a theme, the jazz singer demonstrates his or her jazzness by improvising on every single part of a line, on every single word or non-verbal syllable. When words are involved, this improvisation, this shaping or recasting, affects both the music and the sense of the word. This is the art of jazz vocal phrasing, and this is what defines a jazz singer. Thus, Rainey, Smith, and the others, although they weren't jazz singers strictly speaking, might be said not only to have sung jazz but even to have invented jazz singing—simply because they were the first ones to introduce elements of a jazz posture into their vocal work.

The Blues Shouters
The same was true of the great male "blues shouters"—so named for their firm, full-voiced singing style, a contrast to the rough, sometimes slurred or mumbled delivery of some of the more traditional blues performers. One of the best-known of the early shouters is Big Joe Turner, who came into prominence working with boogie-woogie pianist Pete Johnson in the 1930s, became a popular rhythm-and-blues performer in the 1950s, and later recorded with various ad hoc blues/swing bands. The other is Jimmy Rushing, who sang with the Blue Devils and Bennie Moten's Orchestra in the 1920s but gained his real fame as a longtime member of the Count Basie band, beginning in 1935. Two later exponents of the style were Jimmy Witherspoon, who sang with Jay McShann and had some successes in rhythm-and-blues, and, at a certain period in his career, Ray Charles.

It is a curious fact that most of the really good jazz singers (or singers in jazz) have been female. There have been important exceptions to this rule, including the aforementioned blues shouters, a few big band singers, some of the better bop vocalists, and most notably, a quartet of jazz musicians whose contributions to the music on other instruments is so overwhelming that their vocal work is often overlooked—Louis Armstrong, Jack Teagarden, Fats Waller, and, to a somewhat lesser degree, Dizzy Gillespie.

Female Singers

The greatest, most innovative, most influential singer of the 1930s and 1940s was Billie Holiday. Her voice was modest, but her conception of jazz phrasing was nonpareil, and her ability to affect her audiences with raw emotional power was legendary. Beyond this, her influence on an amazingly large number of jazz and pop singers was as complete and inescapable as Charlie Parker's on saxophonists.

Holiday also was the first important singer, and the most luminous one by far, of what might be called the golden age of jazz singing—the period from the mid-1930s to the mid-1950s in which jazz singing was defined. This music had strong ties to middle-of-the-road pop—most of the songs involved come from the Broadway stage and Tin Pan Alley—but it was altered by a thick jazz atmosphere expressed by various singers through a wide range of vocal textures and rhythmic syntax.

Many of these singers first came to prominence with big bands. Ella Fitzgerald, another of the true innovators of jazz singing, first reached large audiences with Chick Webb's band in the 1930s. She is one of the few singers of the era who owes practically nothing to Billie Holiday, having drawn her inspiration instead from the jazz-like style of the remarkable pop singer Connee Boswell. Sarah Vaughan, perhaps the finest pure *singer* jazz has ever known, was discovered and brought into Earl Hines's band by Billy Eckstine and was later hired by Eckstine for his own famous bop-era band. Helen Humes's rich, bluesy voice was first heard to good advantage with Count Basie. Anita O'Day, a sensuous, reedy singer, was first heard with Gene Krupa and later with Stan Kenton. She influenced June Christy and Chris Connor, who followed her into Kenton's band. Carmen McRae also sings in this style, as do Lorez Alexandria, Dakota Staton, and Nancy Wilson.

Male Singers

Among the male singers who might be appended to this list are several of note. Billy Eckstine was the first of the big-voiced male band singers to achieve wide popularity. Al Hibbler also sang in the big-voiced tradition but his mighty, warbling vibrato sometimes verges on the ludicrous. Joe Williams is an urbane recasting of the blues shouter mold who was featured to fine advantage in Count Basie's band throughout the 1950s. Others are Johnny Hartmann, a fine, confident singer with a deep, sad voice; Earl Coleman, an eloquent ballad singer in the Eckstine tradition; Ernie Andrews, a wonderful, little-known vocalist who also sang in the Eckstine tradition but with a lighter, more engaging sound; and Bill Henderson, whose territory is somewhere between Eckstine's and Joe Williams's. Finally, in a slightly different idiom, there are Nat "King" Cole and Mel Tormé. Cole was a fine, Hines-like pianist and a soft-toned, warm jazz singer before his pop music career took off in the early 1950s, and he maintained more than a little jazz feeling in even his most popular works. Tormé is a careful, able vocalist who uses pop sentimentality to jazz advantage.

Three other very popular male singers should be mentioned

here, because they owe much to jazz. In return, they have influenced jazz singing, although they are not really jazz singers themselves. Bing Crosby sang with Paul Whiteman as one of the "Rhythm Boys" and later recorded with various traditional and swing artists. His slightly hoarse, finely tuned, soft-edged voice inspired several later jazz singers. Tony Bennett uses elements of jazz phrasing in almost all of his work. He has worked with Count Basie and Duke Ellington, among other jazz bandleaders, and has recorded two albums with pianist Bill Evans. Frank Sinatra began his career singing with Harry James and Tommy Dorsey and adapted Billie Holiday-like accents and intonations to the pop big-band format. His talent as a singer is appreciated by all manner of jazz performers who have nothing particular in common with him.

Scat Singing

As big bands and swing gave way to small combos and bop, a curiously attractive vocal device called "scat singing" gained popularity. Scat is consonant-thick, non-verbal singing that employees nonsense syllables like "scop-bop-a-de-bop" or "bing-bang, bing-bang, bing-bang,bing-bang bing-bing-bang, de-deedle-do,bing-bang" to achieve an instrumental-like effect and is usually sung rather fast and percussively.

Scat was hardly a creation of the bop era. It was apparently invented, or at least first used with any regularity and imagination, by Louis Armstrong. Armstrong once said that he started scat singing one night simply because he could not remember the words to the song he was performing. By its very nature, scat implies humor, whether or not it is used for deliberate comic effect, and it was mildly popular during the swing era as a novelty device. Singers like Slim Gaillard (whose big hits were "Flat Foot Floogie" and "Cement Mixer") and Leo Watson anticipated bop uses of scat. Disciples of Watson's like Babs Gonzales, Joe Carroll, and Melvin Moore used scat to bring arcane but energetic humor into bop. Dizzy Gillespie is himself a master of scat singing.

Scat was refined and prettified by Jackie Cain and Roy Kral, a duo who first became popular with saxophonist Charlie Ventura's band. They were by no means exclusively scat singers, but they developed a gentle, almost poignant wordless style for some songs. This style was elaborated later by a French group, the Double Six of Paris, whose album *Bach's Greatest Hits* was popular in the early 1960s.

Vocalese

Another variety of bop singing was an intriguing invention called "vocalese." The idea here was to take not just a melody, but also a good jazz musician's improvisation on a melody, and write stream-of-consciousness words (often a paean to the musician who had created the solo) to it. Leo Watson had worked in this direction, but it seems to have been dancer/singer Eddie Jefferson who first really developed the form. His first successful song of this type was "Moody's Mood for Love," based on a James Moody solo on "I'm in the Mood for Love." Ironically, it was not Jefferson but a singer named Clarence Beeks, self-styled "King Pleasure," who made the song popular. Subsequently, Pleasure wrote good lyrics of this type, and many listeners apparently came to believe that he had invented the form. Vocalese was made slicker and much more successful by a group called Lambert, Hendricks and Ross—Dave Lambert, Jon Hendricks, and Annie Ross. In 1962, Ross was replaced by an actress from Ceylon named Yolande Bavan, who acquitted herself admirably in the group until it disbanded in 1964. Other singers first identified with bop, though not exclusively with either scat or vocalese, include Billy Eckstine and his followers, Jackie Paris, Betty Carter, and, slightly later, Abbey Lincoln.

Few singers were associated with the hard bop or soul jazz movements, although a classically trained vocal conductor named Coleridge Perkinson did arrange some surprisingly successful choral jazz albums for Donald Byrd and Max Roach—the latter featuring Abbey Lincoln.

Recent Developments

There are many other jazz singers of note who are difficult to classify. Mabel Mercer is, strictly speaking, more of a cabaret performer than a jazz singer, but she possesses a refined, extraordinarily moving jazz-influenced delivery and a stunning quality of vocal inflection. Blossom Dearie, who worked with various swing and bop vocal groups in the 1940s and 1950s, is a unique, precious-voiced, jazz-heavy café singer. Nina Simone gave up classical music to become a rocking jazz singer/pianist with a honey-thick voice and strong blues and gospel connections. Cleo Laine has made a number of impeccable, highly polished, rather theatrical jazz albums with her husband, saxophonist John Dankworth. Mose Allison, a good blues/bop pianist and composer of wry, citified blues, is perhaps the most convincing white blues singer in existence. Bob Dorough is a pianist/singer/composer with a strange and wonderful closed-up voice and an amazing manner of pure jazz phrasing.

Perhaps the most successful singer in the avant-garde is Leone Thomas. He has a rich blues voice (he once replaced Joe Williams in Count Basie's orchestra) but is best known for his non-bop scat style which incorporates a kind of Central African yodeling. Another good, but more conventional male vocalist associated with the new music is Andy Bey.

The English singer Norma Winstone and the Polish singer Urszula Dudziak both have extraordinarily pure and powerul voices, and both sing mostly wordless lines that lack even the syllabic structure of scat singing. Dudziak has also been a pioneer in the use of various electronic voice-enhancing instruments and techniques. The Brazilian singer Flora Purim has much of the same purity and power, but she favors a music that is a blend of jazz, Brazilian music, and rather ordinary pop.

Fusion

Among the younger male singers doing interesting things with jazz phrasing are Al Jarreau and Michael Franks, both of whom attempt, with considerable success, to blur the lines between rock and a hip jazz style. Another is Dave Frishberg, a good young pianist and songwriter who sings mostly swing-era material with a voice and inflection somewhere between Bob Dorough and Michael Franks.

Vocals of one sort or another frequently appear on avant-garde and jazz/rock fusion albums, but most of these owe more to commercial rhythm-and-blues styles than to jazz, and the lyrics, when they exist, are almost always tediously obvious.

BESSIE SMITH *(1895–1937)*

Born in Chattanooga, Tennessee, to a life of extreme poverty, Bessie Smith made her stage debut at the age of 9 in an amateur show at the city's Ivory Theatre. Her first professional job came around 1910, when an edition of F. C. Woolcott's "Rabbit Foot Minstrel Show," run by Will "Pa" Rainey and starring his wife Ma Rainey, passed through town. Ma Rainey heard Smith singing and recognized her talent. The young Smith went on the road with the Raineys, singing the era's usual blend of vaudeville tunes, novelty numbers, and stagey blues songs. As she grew, both physically and in confidence and skill, Smith became dissatisfied with the show, and she soon struck out on her own.

She spent the next few years working clubs and dance halls throughout the South. During this period, she met two men who were later to affect her career—a promoter named Frank Walker and the fine New Orleans pianist and songwriter Clarence Williams. In 1920, Smith made her first records, for the Emerson Recording Company (they were never released and the masters have been lost). Working with Williams and other accompanists and integrating dance routines and male impersonations into her act, Smith became one of the most popular entertainers on the Southern circuit. Although she continued to perform several kinds of music in her shows, it was her frank, earthy, but sophisticated blues that audiences grew to love above all else.

In 1921, Smith toured Ohio and Illinois with Sidney Bechet in a show called *How Come* that featured Bechet as a Chinese laundryman of the same name. It closed when it reached New York, but Clarence Williams arranged for Smith to make a test record with Bechet and cornetist Bubber Miley while she was in the city. It was rejected by the record company, Okeh, but it set the stage for her recording career. The next year, Smith moved to Philadelphia. While she was there, Frank Walker, who had been hired by Columbia Records to supervise their "race records," sent Williams to find her and bring her back to New York.

In 1923, Smith cut her first sides for Columbia with Williams and another pianist named Irving Johns. From then until 1929, she recorded and toured prolifically, working with musicians like Louis Armstrong and Fletcher Henderson. On one occasion she led a sextet that included Coleman Hawkins, clarinetist Buster Bailey, and trombonist Charlie Green, a frequent associate of Smith's. She also worked with pianist Porter Grainger and James P. Johnson during this period.

In the late 1920s, Smith's recording career faltered. This was apparently due in part to the public's satiation with the kind of music she performed, and partly it was a result of personal problems that included alcoholism and a temperamental disloyalty to old friends and colleagues. In 1929, she appeared in a short film based on W. C. Handy's "St. Louis Blues," and she made a handful of recordings in 1930 and 1931, including two gospel songs with a vocal quartet; but for most of that period, she worked in roadshows and small clubs when she worked at all. In 1933, she made her last records, with Jack Teagarden, Benny Goodman, Chu Berry, and trumpeter Frank Newton.

In her final years, Smith's fortunes rose slightly and then fell hard. She worked in low-class nightclubs, sang for private parties, and even sold chewing gum in a theatre. An engagement at Connie's Inn in New York in 1936 was moderately successful, and in 1937, there was talk of another recording session and perhaps a stage show.

In late September of that year, on her way to an engagement in the South, Smith was killed in an automobile accident in Mississippi. There are conflicting stories about her final hours, but it seems possible that she either was refused admittance to a nearby hospital because she was black or was allowed to bleed to death by doctors who were more concerned with the white victims of the crash.

Bessie Smith was a remarkable singer, with a pure, direct, honest delivery and a great, seemingly unforced sensuality. She phrased her words with great care, sliding and bending notes to precisely the right point for whatever effect she wanted to achieve and holding on to each syllable with bulldog tenacity until she was good and ready to let it go. Her vocal technique, coupled with the natural radiance of her voice, gave unparalleled strength to whatever she sang.

Selected Recordings

Any Woman's Blues (two-record set, Columbia)
Empty Bed Blues (two-record set, Columbia)
The Empress (two-record set, Columbia)
Nobody's Blues but Mine (two-record set, Columbia)
World's Greatest Blues Singer (two-record set, Columbia)

These Columbia LPs, all of which are two-record sets issued in the 1970s, represent virtually a complete set of the recordings of Bessie Smith, from the first ones in 1923 with Clarence Williams and Irving Johns to the final session in 1933. Most of Smith's recordings were accompanied by piano and one or two other instruments, and more than one otherwise undistinguished trombonist, trumpeter, or saxophonist seems to have been stirred to great heights as he provided insinuating, sinuous obbligatos to Smith's rich voice. It is difficult to single out one of the five sets as the best, but a good starting place might be *Empty Bed Blues,* which includes the blatantly sexual title song and such other Smith classics as "Ticket Agent, Ease Your Window Down," "I'd Rather Be Dead and Buried in My Grave," and "Me and My Gin"—all from 1924 or 1928.

BILLIE HOLIDAY   *(Eleanor Gough) (1915–59)*

The illegitimate daughter of guitarist Clarence Holiday (who played with Fletcher Henderson and Don Redman, among others), Baltimore-born Eleanor (or Eleanora) Gough was dubbed "Billie" by her mother in honor of actress Billie Dove. When Holiday was still young, her mother moved to New York to look for work, and the child was left with relatives. She did housework and ran errands for a brothel to make money, and when her mother brought her to New York around 1928, Holiday went to work as a prostitute in a local brothel. Almost at once, she was arrested, and she spent four months in jail on Welfare Island.

Upon her release, she was desperate for money. She had begun singing at this time, and, having talked her way into an audition at the Log Cabin Club in Harlem, she got a job singing for tips. Soon, she was being paid a regular salary to sing at other clubs in the neighborhood, and at one of these, in 1933, she was heard by John Hammond, who was impressed enough with her to arrange for her to record with Benny Goodman. Soon, she was working at better clubs and appearing at the Apollo Theatre, Harlem's most important musical showcase.

Holiday began recording with various small groups, most of them led by Teddy Wilson and including such stars as Ben Webster, Lester Young, Roy Eldridge, and two of the stars of the Duke Ellington reed section, Harry Carney and Johnny Hodges. These early recordings are perhaps her finest work. She sang briefly with the Jimmie Lunceford and Fletcher Henderson bands, and then joined Count Basie for about a year in 1937. She rarely recorded with Basie (they were under contract to different record labels), and she recorded only minimally with Artie Shaw's band, the next one that she joined.

In 1939, Holiday had a long engagement at Barney Josephson's famous Greenwich Village club, Café Society. Throughout the 1940s, she sang at many top clubs and theatres in New York, Chicago, and Los Angeles. She had a number of hit records, including versions of "Lover Man," "Strange Fruit" (based on a grim Lewis Allan poem about lynchings in the South), "God Bless the Child" (which Holiday herself wrote the words for), and "Gloomy Sunday" (the "Hungarian suicide song" first popularized by Paul Whiteman). Holiday's version of this last song was banned from the airwaves, because it apparently inspired several unhappy souls to take their own lives. She also starred in a mediocre Hollywood musical called *New Orleans* (1947).

Although her career thrived in these years, Holiday's personal life was in extreme disrepair. She drank heavily, had become a heroin addict, and had a string of unhappy love affairs—all of which not only ruined her health (and eventually her voice), but also kept her almost permanently in need of money. In mid-1947, she was arrested for narcotics violations in Philadelphia and sent to a federal reformatory for some months. Upon her release, she returned to an active performance schedule of concerts and club dates, including several European tours. From 1956 on, she seems to have given up narcotics (at least most of the time), but she compensated by becoming an even heavier drinker. Inevitably, her health failed completely.

In May 1959, Holiday made her last public appearance, at the Phoenix Theatre in New York (she was forbidden to appear in clubs in New York City because of her narcotics arrests). In June, she collapsed and was taken to the hospital, where she died ten weeks later. According to some reports, she was under arrest at the time of her death for alleged possession of dangerous drugs.

As the tragic geniuses of jazz go, Holiday was one of the most tragic, one of the greatest geniuses. She was an artist who could completely transform her material, transcending it when necessary and enriching it always. She had a way of shaping songs into a fiercely personal statement of her own feelings—sometimes literally rewriting the melody to fit her sense of emotional dynamics. She had a consummate knowledge of jazz phrasing, which she applied in an instrumental-like way to whatever she sang and an almost mysterious manner of making songs live, seem true. No other singer could do what she did. Luckily for the state of jazz singing, many singers have tried.

Selected Recordings

Billie Holiday: The Golden Years (three-record set, Columbia)
Strange Fruit (Atlantic)
The Billie Holiday Story (Decca)
Stormy Blues (two-record set, Verve)

The excellent Columbia set dates from 1933 (with Benny

Goodman) to 1941 (with Teddy Wilson), and includes several rare tracks of Holiday with the Count Basie band. Lester Young and Roy Eldridge are among the musicians. The Atlantic album, originally recorded for the Commodore label in 1944, is prime. Holiday appears with trumpeter Frank Newton's orchestra (including alto saxophonist Tab Smith) and with groups led by pianist Eddie Heywood, and she is in fine condition. The Decca recordings feature Holiday with Bobby Hackett and Louis Armstrong, and, on some tracks, show a clear lessening of vocal power.

The Verve LP, a two-record set, is from 1954 and 1955. It features many good musicians (trumpeters Harry "Sweets" Edison and Charlie Shavers, saxophonists Willie Smith, Benny Carter, and Budd Johnson, pianists Carl Drinkard and Jimmy Rowles) and is composed almost entirely of good-quality standards ("I Thought About You," "Everything Happens to Me," "I Don't Stand a Ghost of a Chance with You"). It shows Holiday in reasonably good voice but is an illustration of what a once-great singer sounds like when she is merely getting by.

ELLA FITZGERALD *(1918–   )*

Ella Fitzgerald was born in Newport News, Virginia. Her parents died when she was quite young, and she went to live in New York City with her aunt. She had started singing informally at an early age, and, as a teenager in New York, she began entering amateur contests. In 1934, at 16, she won one of these—the Harlem Amateur Hour—and almost immediately she was hired by Chick Webb, one of the best of the powerhouse swing drummers, to join his excellent big band.

With Fitzgerald in the front ranks, the band played throughout most of the late 1930s at the renowned Savoy Ballroom ("Stompin' at the Savoy," which Webb helped to write, became something of a swing-era anthem). Fitzgerald's first recording with Webb was "Love and Kisses" in 1935, but her biggest hit by far in this era was "A-Tisket A-Tasket," arranged by Van Alexander in 1938. Fitzgerald had married Webb, and when he died of tuberculosis in 1939, she took over leadership of the group, holding it together for more than two years. After that time, she broke it up, in order to pursue her own career.

Fitzgerald had earned such a good reputation as a singer in her relatively short stay with the Webb band that she was able to find work at once as a solo performer. Since that time, although she has recorded and appeared with Duke Ellington and other noted bandleaders, she has never found it necessary to work with anybody else's group for any length of time. In the mid-1940s, she started a series of tours with Jazz at the Philharmonic and also began to tour extensively on her own. Until 1955, almost all of her records were on the Decca label, and that company encouraged her to become more and more of a mainstream pop singer. When she left Decca to join the more jazz-oriented Verve label, for whom she made most of her best mature recordings, she was a well-known singer to both pop and jazz audiences. Her reputation was enhanced by television appearances, occasional film roles (most notably in *Pete Kelly's Blues*), engagements in Las Vegas, and a continued formidable schedule of European, Asian, and North and South American touring.

In 1971, she had serious eye trouble, which curtailed her activities for several years until successful operations restored her health. Since 1972, she has appeared with symphony orchestras and jazz groups such as Count Basie's band and Oscar Peterson's trio. She has also made a series of jazz-backed recordings for the Pablo label, often with guitarist Joe Pass and/or her accompanist of more than a decade, the superb pianist Tommy Flanagan. She remains active and sometimes seems to be regaining some of the pure jazz feeling she has integrated into pop music for much of her career.

Fitzgerald has had so much success in the popular arena that it is easy to forget how firmly grounded in jazz she is. She refashions or recasts a song less than some other singers like Billie Holiday or Carmen McRae. Her jazz inflection is more subtle, and she seems more concerned with reading a song with jazz accents than translating it into jazz. There is also less raw emotional content in her singing than there is in Holiday's and that of Holiday's successors—although this is not to suggest that Fitzgerald is in any way cold. It's just that she tends to let songs, especially good songs, speak for themselves. She does this with a voice that is extraordinarily clear and precisely formed—a voice that might best be described simply as elegant. She has not spawned hosts of imitators, nor has she changed the course of jazz singing as Bessie Smith and Holiday did; but it is doubtful that a songwriter has ever had a better friend in the world of jazz.

Selected Recordings

The Best of Chick Webb and His Orchestra (two-record set, MCA)
The Best of Ella (two-record set, MCA)
The Rodgers and Hart Songbook (two-record set, Verve)
The Duke Ellington Songbook (two-record set, Verve)
Take Love Easy (Pablo)

The MCA albums, both two-record sets recently reissued, are material originally released on Decca. The Webb sides feature ten tracks with Fitzgerald, including "A-Tisket A-Tasket," "The Dipsy Doodle," and " 'Taint What You Do." The band tracks feature such strong soloists as trumpeter Taft Jordan and saxophonists Hilton Jefferson and Wayman Carver—the latter of whom was also the first real jazz flautist. They also are very good listening. There is a bit of duplication on the other MCA album ("A-Tisket A-Tasket" and one other song with Webb), but it is, in general, devoted to Fitzgerald's post-Webb days with Decca, through 1955. Sy Oliver's orchestra is involved, as are the Ink Spots and the Delta Rhythm Boys, and the material ranges from the amusing ("It's Only a Paper Moon" with the latter vocal group) to the ridiculous ("Tender Trap"). The Rodgers and Hart set of two records is one of a series of albums devoted to top composers that Fitzgerald recorded for Verve in the 1950s. The others are devoted to Cole Porter, George and Ira Gershwin, Jerome Kern, and Harold Arlen, and there is also a wonderful version of "Porgy and Bess" with Louis Armstrong. All of these are well worth hearing, but the Rodgers and Hart set, featuring the Buddy Bregman orchestra, is particularly inspired—at least partially because the songs themselves are so strong.

Despite its title, the Ellington set (also two records) is not exactly one of the regular "Songbook" recordings. It was, instead, originally issued as part of a four-record Duke-and-Ella project, half of which featured Fitzgerald with various small bands (usually including Oscar Peterson) doing well-known Ellington or Ellington-associated songs like "Mood Indigo" and "Sophisticated Lady." The set at hand is the other half of the project, with Fitzgerald actually singing with the Ellington band (augmented by occasional guests, including Dizzy Gillespie on one track, saxophonist Frank Foster—who properly belonged in Count Basie's band at the time—throughout, and Billy Strayhorn on piano on one side). The material includes popular Ellington songs like "I Got It Bad and That Ain't Good," "I'm Beginning to See the Light," "Take the 'A' Train," "I Ain't Got Nothing But the Blues," and "I Didn't Know About You," plus some lesser-known works, and concludes with a four-part "Portrait of Ella Fitzgerald," narrated by Ellington and Strayhorn. Fitzgerald is in fine form and includes plenty of her pure, lighthearted scat singing where appropriate.

The Atlantic LP, from 1972, offers new versions of some of the songs on the Porter "Songbook," with a few others added. Some of the grace is gone from Fitzgerald's voice by this time, but she still sings well and with obvious affection for the material. The Pablo album, on which Fitzgerald is accompanied only by guitarist Joe Pass, is a warm but almost sedate album packed with exceptionally good songs (Ellington's "Take Love Easy," Strayhorn's "Lush Life"—the best torch song ever written—Don Redman's "Gee Baby, Ain't I Good to You," Billy Eckstine's "I Want to Talk About You," and Ord Hamilton's "You're Blasé," among others). It lacks some of the rousing excitement of some of Fitzgerald's other Pablo recordings, but her voice is calm and confident.

SARAH VAUGHAN *(1924–   )*

Sarah Vaughan's first public appearances as a singer came in the choir of the Baptist church her family attended in Newark, New Jersey, where she was born. She had originally wanted to be a pianist and studied that instrument for nearly ten years as a child and teenager. In 1942, she won an amateur contest at the Apollo Theatre in Harlem and, through this came to the attention of Billy Eckstine. Eckstine had been the vocalist with Earl Hines's superlative band since 1939; it was he who convinced Hines to hire Vaughan as a second vocalist and second pianist. When Eckstine left the band and organized his own unit in 1944, Vaughan was his star vocalist. That same year, she made her first records in a session produced by jazz critic Leonard Feather for the Continental label, now long defunct.

Leaving Eckstine in 1945, Vaughan appeared briefly with bassist John Kirby's highly appreciated small band and then launched a successful career. She was one of the few vocalists of the era, if not the only one, who seemed to understand intuitively the rhythmic and harmonic implications of bop. This endeared her to Parker, Gillespie, Powell, and other jazz stars of the era, and they worked with her and helped her to find other jobs. In 1947, she married trumpeter George Treadwell, and he took over management of her career. Throughout the late 1940s, the 1950s, and most of the 1960s, she recorded extensively for Columbia, Mercury, and EmArcy.

Although Vaughan has recorded her share of mediocre popular material (including an album of Henry Mancini songs and one devoted to the works of Michel Legrand), she has usually remained closer to pure jazz than many of her colleagues have. This is certainly due, at least in part, to the fact that her conception of the vocal art is so closely tied to bop and post-bop improvisational ideas. She reworks melodies in the most imaginative ways, building on them rather than simply changing them as some singers do. Moreover, she does this with one of the most remarkable voices that any sort of popular music has ever known—one that is rich and powerful, thick with character, capable of the most astonishing highs and lows, full of subtlety and sensitivity, and nearly always brimming over with an unforced sense of smoldering passion. Many of her devices—her purring portamento, her surprising octave jumps, the way she has of somehow making her vocal lines sing obbligatos to themselves—have been widely copied, though never with much success. She is astonishing.

Selected Recordings

Sarah Vaughan (Everest)
Sarah Vaughan Recorded Live (two-record set, EmArcy)
Send in the Clowns (Mainstream)
Sarah Vaughan: Duke Ellington; Song Book One (Pablo)

The Everest LP includes good bop-era jazz like Vaughan's classic 1945 recording of "Lover Man" with Parker, Gillespie, and Al Haig; several tracks with Teddy Wilson or Bud Powell; some recordings with George Treadwell from 1946–48; and Vaughan's version of "Nature Boy."

The live set, two records, dates from 1957–63 and was recorded at four different concert dates, from Chicago to Copenhagen. Some of the tracks are with a small band led by cornetist Thad Jones, and others are with trios featuring pianists Ronnel Bright and Kirk Stuart. The Mainstream album is an example of good pop-oriented Vaughan. Like Ella Fitzgerald, Vaughan has recorded numerous LPs featuring the works of a single songwriter—although Vaughan's have lacked the singlemindness of tone that Fitzgerald's usually have. The Ellington album is newly recorded (in 1979) and shows the singer in stunningly good form. The musicians include saxophonists Zoot Sims, Frank Foster, and Frank Wess; trumpeter Waymon Reed; trombonist J. J. Johnson (in a rare recent record appearance); pianists Jimmy Rowles and Mike Wofford; and guitarists Joe Pass and Bucky Pizzarelli. Among the songs are "I'm Just a Lucky So-and-So," "Lush Life," "Sophisticated Lady," and a definitive version of "Solitude."

EDDIE JEFFERSON *(1918–79)*

Eddie Jefferson was born in Pittsburgh, and from an early age, he was encouraged by his musician father to develop his own talents as an instrumentalist (he chose tuba), singer, and dancer. When he was about 15, he began appearing professionally. One of his first jobs was at the Chicago World's Fair in 1933, and later he worked with an orchestra led by Coleman Hawkins. Through the 1940s and 1950s, he developed a steady, if not exactly distinguished, career, working (mostly as a dancer) with radio star Lanny Ross's concert tours and with a stage show starring Sarah Vaughan, among other things.

In about 1938 or 1939, he started singing along with instrumental records for his friends' amusement, making up lyrics as he went along. In the 1940s, with his dance partner of the time, Irv Taylor, he began incorporating the device into a stage show, formalizing the lyrics that he had made up. In 1951 or 1952, singer Clarence Beeks (known professionally as King Pleasure) heard Jefferson's words to James Moody's solo on the Jimmy McHugh/Dorothy Fields song "I'm in the Mood for Love" and liked the idea well enough to record his interpretation of the transmuted standard. It was something of a hit and led to the modest popularization of "vocalese," as the process came to be called, by Pleasure and later by Lambert, Hendricks and Ross. Jefferson made his own first recordings in the early 1950s, but he never achieved the acclaim gained by Pleasure, and other performers in the style.

In 1953, Jefferson joined Moody, who had been one of his main inspirations, as a vocalist and band manager. He continued the association, off and on, until the early 1960s. He returned briefly to dancing as a career but then rejoined Moody for another five years or so. In 1974, he started working with a group called Artistic Truth, led by Moody's former drummer, Roy Brooks.

In 1976, Jefferson began a new series of solo recordings for the Muse and Inner City labels and undertook tours of leading American jazz clubs. In 1979, outside a club in Detroit, in the midst of one of these tours, he was shot to death by an unknown assailant.

It has often been said that Jefferson never received the credit that he deserved for inventing vocalese. That is certainly true, but it is even more disappointing that he has been given still less credit for being a fine overall jazz singer. Vocalese was a minor, if enjoyable, musical invention, a gimmick that brought humor and even some measure of literary insight to jazz improvisation. Jefferson's contribution to jazz went far beyond that: his hardy, almost heroic voice was among the most musicianly that jazz has ever known—agile, intense, magnificently modulated. In addition, he probably came closer to emulating the jazz sense of the saxophonists he based many of his lines on (Parker, Hawkins, Lester Young, Dexter Gordon, and so on) than any other non-saxophonist has ever done.

Selected Recordings

The Bebop Singers by Eddie Jefferson, Joe Carroll, and Annie Ross (Prestige)
The Jazz Singer (Inner City)
Body and Soul (Prestige)
Things Are Getting Better (Muse)
Still on the Planet (Muse)

The Prestige anthology has only four Jefferson tracks dating from his second recording session (1953). They feature rather too much foolishness with Irv Taylor, but they show the singer's beginnings, and the material by other singers is worth hearing, too. Especially notable is Annie Ross's classic original vocalese versions of "Twisted" and "Farmer's Market." The Inner City LP is a reissue of material that was originally recorded in 1959 and 1961 for the obscure Triumph label and mostly features Moody and trumpeters Johnny Coles or Howard McGhee. Included are versions of "Body and Soul," "Moody's Mood for Love" (as the "I'm in the Mood for Love" variation was called), and Horace Silver's "Sister Sadie." There are also tracks of Miles Davis's "So What?" (turned into an apologia for the trumpeter's habit of turning his back on audiences or leaving the stage while other musicians were soloing) and "Honeysuckle Rose." *Body and Soul* stars Jefferson's popular 1969 version of the song. The first Muse album includes vocalese versions of such comparatively advanced songs as Miles Davis's "Bitches' Brew" and Eddie Harris's "Freedom Jazz Dance" and is kicked along by an excellent modern/mainstream small band, including trumpeter Joe Newman, tenor saxophonist Billy Mitchell, and pianist Mickey Tucker. The band on the second Muse album includes Tucker again, fusion bassist Rick Laird, trumpeter Waymon Reed, and alto saxophonist Richie Cole. It is less coherent than that on the first Muse, but Jefferson is in top voice, working his way through Benny Harris's bop classic "Ornithology," "I Got the Blues" (Jefferson's version of "Lester Leaps In"), Hank Crawford's "Sherry" (formerly a vehicle for Ray Charles's alto saxophone), and some energetic originals.

-7-

Hors Concourse: Duke Ellington and Miles Davis

azz lovers who claim they don't think much of Duke Ellington are like professors of English who disparage Shakespeare or Dickens: they're either malcontents who will have nothing to do with greatness, no matter what anybody says, or they are over-impressed with their own cleverness.

With Miles Davis, the situation is somewhat different: there are plenty of honest jazz fans who simply do not care much for his music—or who may like his music from some periods but wouldn't want to hear him play in all of his many, steadily progressive stylistic guises.

Nevertheless, both men are among the most important, artistically successful, and highly skilled American musicians of the 20th century, and it would not be easy to say which of the two has had more influence on the shape of jazz today. If Ellington is more universally loved than Davis, it may be only because he created an oeuvre that was so completely his own, so brilliantly original, and, even at its most complex, so wonderfully accessible that he was never a threat (for long) to the musical traditions he drew from and enhanced. It was the nature of Davis's genius, on the other hand (and will surely be again, if he ever emerges from his self-imposed retirement), to disrupt the jazz flow, to ask embarrassing questions, to stir up musical trouble. While Ellington would gush, "I love you madly" from the bandstand in fourteen languages, Davis would scowl and slouch and look as if he were about to spit. Ellington's music embraced the world; Davis's challenged it.

Ellington and Davis each professed great respect for the other's music, but they never worked together. They might well have done so. Some of Davis's best and best-known recordings were with big bands whose textures were not unlike Ellington's; Ellington recorded with great success as a pianist with bop and post-bop musicians (including Max Roach, Charles Mingus, and a pre-revolutionary John Coltrane). Still, it is difficult to imagine a collaboration between the two men. By the time they might have joined forces, each had developed such unshakeable ideas about his own music, and about music in general, that it may well have been impossible for them to have met on common ground.

If Ellington and Davis are difficult to classify, if they seem to demand a place of their own in the jazz pantheon, it is due as much to their tendentiousness, their sense of hard-held musical conviction, as it is to their considerable musical abilities. Moreover, this skill and this tendentiousness were coupled with long creative careers (roughly fifty years in Ellington's case, roughly thirty years, so far, in Davis's) that made it possible for each to develop his musical individualism.

Of course, it is possible to describe in general terms the musical place of Ellington and Davis: The former was an original (if stride-influenced) pianist who led what became an early swing band and grew into a highly versatile mainstream group with plenty of classical and more modern overtones; the latter was an excellent bop trumpeter who evolved into a major innovator of cool jazz, post-bop, the avant-garde, and fusion.

Nevertheless, neither man fits comfortably in the same field with other important jazz musicians. This may be true because, in the jazz arena, neither man plays fair: Davis breaks the rules, questions the premises, then lets the new rules rewrite themselves; Ellington owns the game.

DUKE ELLINGTON *(Edward Kennedy Ellington)*
(1899– 1974)

It is said that Edward Kennedy Ellington, who was born into a comfortable middle-class family in Washington, D.C., earned his noble nickname when he was about 8 years old, courtesy of a neighbor who was impressed with his personal bearing. This aristocratic style seems to have developed rather earlier than his interest in music, however: he took piano lessons as a youth, but didn't take to the piano.

When he went to Armstrong High School, one of the area's best-known black educational institutions, his first interest was art. He was talented enough to be offered a scholarship to Brooklyn's noted Pratt Institute later on, but he refused it. Meanwhile, his interest in music slowly grew, and he began to study it both at the high school and privately.

Soon Ellington was playing informally at rent parties and local clubs, apparently in the style of the stride and later ragtime pianists who were so popular in the vicinity at the time. Around the same period, while still in high school, he also took a part-time job in a soda fountain, an experience that inspired his first composition, "Soda Fountain Rag." He left Armstrong before graduation and ran his own sign-painting business for a time. Gradually, he started getting regular jobs as a pianist in a variety of Washington area clubs and theatres. Sometimes, he worked as a solo performer, but when he worked with local bands, his associates often included two other young Washington musicians with whom he had earlier shared a music teacher—saxophonist Otto Hardwicke and trumpeter Arthur Whetsol.

In 1919, too, Ellington joined with Hardwicke and Whetsol to form his first band, which he dubbed "The Duke's Serenaders." Shortly thereafter, drummer Sonny Greer was added to the ensemble, and the Serenaders began to earn a name for themselves as a good young dance band. In 1922, led by Elmer Snowden, who played the banjo and its cousin the banjorine, the group went to New York briefly to play with clarinetist Wilbur Sweatman's band. They returned to Washington, under the name "The Washingtonians," and under Snowden's leadership, worked for a short time in Atlantic City before going back to New York—this time at the behest of Fats Waller, whom Ellington and his friends had met and listened to on their first visit to Manhattan. Late in 1923, the band began a residency at New York's Hollywood Club—later renamed the Kentucky Club—that was to last, off and on, through late 1927.

Snowden left the band in 1924 and was replaced by banjoist Fred Guy (who later took up the guitar as well). Ellington resumed leadership of the group, and, ever more successful, it gradually increased in size. Whetsol returned to Washington to study medicine (although he later rejoined the band several times), and his place was taken by Bubber Miley. Louis Metcalf was added as second trumpet. Henry "Bass" Edwards signed on to play bass and tuba but left after about a year. He was then replaced by Wellman Braud, who was in turn replaced by *two* bassists when he left. Charlie Irvis joined as trombonist and was subsequently supplanted by Joe "Tricky Sam" Nanton. Harry Carney, whose specialty was the baritone saxophone, and Rudy Jackson were added to the reed section.

The new personnel—especially Miley, Carney, and the two trombonists—changed the band immeasurably. It became earthier, more blues-conscious, less saccharine; more of a jazz band, less of a dance band. It also began to develop for the first time the tonal patterns, concepts of horn voicing, and particular rhythmic sense that helped to define the band, in one form or another, from that time on.

Discovery and the Cotton Club

In 1927, Ellington was "discovered" by entrepreneur Irving Mills, who became his manager for some years and set about trying to make him an international celebrity. Much has been said about Mills, pro and con: for instance, he received a composer's credit, and presumably publishing royalties as well, on many of Ellington's songs, although he was not a musician at all. Whatever role he played, he undeniably had a great beneficial influence on Ellington's career. The first thing he did was to arrange for Ellington's debut recording, on which the band cut a rendition of the now classic "Black and Tan Fantasy," co-authored by Ellington and Bubber Miley. He also got the band booked into the Cotton Club in Harlem, the best-known and most elaborate of the New York clubs then offering black entertainment to well-heeled white audiences.

Ellington's stay at the Cotton Club lasted until 1931. The band grew in size and sophistication, despite the fact that much of their music was geared to feverishly imaginative floor shows—the source of the band's growling, percussive "jungle music." It was this engagement, enhanced by outside concerts, continued recordings, and frequent nationwide radio broadcasts, that initially made the reputation of the Duke Ellington orchestra.

During this period, the noted New Orleans clarinetist Barney Bigard joined Ellington, and Arthur Whetsol returned to the fold. Louis Metcalf left and was replaced by Freddy Jenkins, and Bubber Miley gave way to Cootie Williams. Juan Tizol joined as second trombonist. However, the most significant addition to the band, by far, was Johnny Hodges, who replaced Otto Hardwicke and was to become not only the most brilliant saxophonist (on soprano and, mostly, alto saxophone) in Ellington's generally brilliant saxophone section, but one of the three or four greatest saxophonists jazz has ever known. His tone was elegant, sweet, and ethereally pure, and his versatile imagination apparently inexhaustible. The band also had its first popular hit, a version of "Mood Indigo" (at first called "Dreamy Blues") while at the Cotton Club. This was certainly, in both artistic and commercial terms, the first of the Ellington organization's many golden eras.

Ellington the Composer

When the band left the Cotton Club in 1931, it was famous and much in demand. For several years, Ellington toured the country and played engagements at many of the top theatres of the day, in New York and elsewhere. Ellington was well into his astonishingly prolific composing career by this time, having already written or co-written more than fifty works—among them "East St. Louis Toodle-oo" (which became the band's theme), "The Mooch," "Rockin' in Rhythm," "Sophisticated Lady," and "It Don't Mean a Thing (If It Ain't Got That Swing)," in addition to "Mood Indigo" and "Black and Tan Fantasy." Not only did many of these works have popular success, but they attracted the attention of serious musicians as well. The noted Australian pianist and composer Percy Grainger found elements of J. S. Bach and (more obviously) Frederick Delius in Ellington's compositions; others mentioned Igor Stravinsky, Claude Debussy, and Maurice Ravel.

Throughout the 1930s, the band worked constantly, touring the United States, Canada, and Europe and playing several return engagements at the Cotton Club. Among the more notable additions to the band during these years were trombonist Lawrence Brown, Ivie Anderson as vocalist, and Rex Stewart on cornet. The end of the decade saw three more particularly important additions. The first was tenor saxophonist Ben Webster, the band's first soloist on that instrument, which produced a rich, grumbling tone that added further depth to the band's already superb reed sound. The second, bassist Jimmy Blanton, virtually invented the modern jazz bass, despite a tragically short life. Finally, and most important of all, there was pianist/composer/arranger Billy Strayhorn, whose fertile musical imagination was so much like Ellington's that he had the effect of doubling Ellington's strengths, and who wrote or co-wrote such classic Ellingtonia as "Lush Life," "Take the 'A' Train" (which supplanted "East St. Louis Toodle-oo" as the band's theme), "Chelsea Bridge," "Passion Flower," "A Drum is a Woman," and "Such Sweet Thunder." From the time these last three men joined the band until 1942, when a recording ban was imposed by the musicians' union, Ellington recorded what was to remain some of his best work.

In 1943, Ellington was honored with a "Duke Ellington

Week" celebrating the twentieth anniversary of his first appearance in New York. The band, with some further personnel changes (most notably the replacement of Cootie Williams by trumpeter/violinist/vocalist Ray Nance), performed at Carnegie Hall, presenting, among other things, Ellington's first extended work, "Black, Brown and Beige." The Carnegie Hall concert was to become an annual event for some years, and Ellington was to continue to compose longer, more ambitious works for these and other similar appearances—among them, "The Liberian Suite," "New World A-Comin'," and "The Tattooed Bride."

Despite some slack years in the early 1950s, when the band seemed to lose some of its creative momentum, the next two decades were a period of almost non-stop, high-quality performing and recording by Ellington and his group. Among the compositions that Ellington wrote or co-wrote during this period were "Do Nothin' Till You Hear from Me" (originally called "Concerto for Cootie"), "I Ain't Got Nothin' but the Blues," "I'm Beginning to See the Light," "Creole Rhapsody," "All Too Soon," "I Got It Bad (And That Ain't Good)," "Things Ain't What They Used To Be," "Don't Get Around Much Anymore," "Don't You Know I Care," "I Didn't Know About You," "I'm Just a Lucky So-and-So," "Just Squeeze Me," "It Shouldn't Happen to a Dream," "Satin Doll," and "I'm Gonna Go Fishin' " (the theme from *Anatomy of a Murder,* for which Ellington wrote his first film score).

Personnel Changes

The personnel continued to change, most dramatically in 1951, when Sonny Greer (who had been with Ellington for thirty years), Johnny Hodges, and Lawrence Brown all gave notice. (Hodges led his own band until 1955, then returned to the Ellington orchestra, where he remained until his death in 1970; Brown returned in 1960, staying until 1970.) Among the musicians who joined Ellington over this span of time were trumpeters Willie Cook, Taft Jordan, Cat Anderson (who remained with the band, off and on, until 1971), Clark Terry, Harold Baker, and (briefly) Dizzy Gillespie. On saxophone, there were Al Sears, Hilton Jefferson, Don Byas, Willie Smith, Russell Procope, and Jimmy Hamilton (who both became permanent fixtures in the band, doubling on saxophone and clarinet). Saxophonist Paul Gonsalves joined in 1950 and stayed for almost twenty-five years, becoming the band's longest-tenured tenor saxophonist by far and covering the ample middle ground between Carney and Hodges with consummate skill. Well-known trombonists were Wilbur De Paris, Tyree Glenn (who doubled on vibraharp), Quentin Jackson, and Britt Woodman. Also featured were bassists Oscar Pettiford, Wendell Marshall, John Lamb, Jimmy Woode, and Aaron Bell; drummers Butch Ballard, Louis Bellson, and Sam Woodyard; and vocalists Kay Davis, Al Hibbler, Herb Jeffries, and Betty Roche.

In the 1960s, the band continued to operate as a full-time performing and recording unit. It was in many ways the best Ellington band of all, thanks to the perfection of Hodges, Gonsalves, Carney, Hamilton, and Procope in the reed section—

which remained intact from the mid-1950s to the late 1960s—and to the continued good services of Lawrence Brown, Cat Anderson, Ray Nance, and Cootie Williams (who had left the band in 1940, inspiring pianist Raymond Scott to pen a mournful tribute called "When Cootie Left the Duke," and returned in 1962). However, Ellington himself embarked on numerous other projects as well. He wrote and recorded two more film scores (*Paris Blues* and *Assault on a Queen*) and composed a number of extended works, including "Impressions of the Far East," "Virgin Islands Suite," "Suite Thursday," "The Golden Broom and the Green Apple" (commissioned by the New York Philharmonic Orchestra), and "Latin American Suite." He created incidental music for a production of *Timon of Athens* at the Stratford (Ontario) Shakespeare Festival and for a stage work in honor of the 100th anniversary of the Emancipation Proclamation. He wrote words and music for the first two of his three "Sacred Concerts" (the first of them performed in San Francisco's Grace Cathedral in 1965). He made a number of small-band long-playing records with musicians he was not ordinarily associated with, including Charles Mingus and Max Roach, John Coltrane, Coleman Hawkins, and Stéphane Grappelli. In 1965, the music jury for the Pulitzer Prize unanimously recommended that Ellington be given the award, but the Pulitzer Advisory Board rejected the recommendation—prompting Ellington to observe, "Fate is being kind to me. Fate doesn't want me to be famous too young."

The Later Years

Into the 1970s (and into his own 70s), Ellington continued to be as active as ever. He wrote more extended works ("The New Orleans Suite," "The River"—a suite written for the American Ballet Theatre—"Afro-Eurasian Eclipse," "The Goutelas Suite," "Togo Brava Suite," and others) as well as conventional shorter pieces and led his orchestra around the United States and to Europe, the Soviet Union, Australia, and Asia.

Ellington's health failed early in 1974, and he was able to join his band on tour only occasionally. In May of that year, less than two months after his 75th birthday, he died of lung cancer and pneumonia. His son Mercer, who had been road manager for the band as well as a member of its trumpet section since 1965, took over leadership immediately and has continued to lead it since that time—although there has been virtually a complete change in personnel.

His Contributions

Ellington's greatest contribution to jazz was his orchestra. It was a mighty thing, continually growing, refining itself, advancing onto new terrain. Although it incorporated many kinds of music into its vocabulary, it was somehow oblivious to the trends of the moment. When it commented upon them directly, it was usually with wit and even a touch of condescension. It was its own creature—or, rather, Ellington's, for he led the band with an all-encompassing sense of purpose and direction. The band was full of highly individualistic players, original solo voices who had their own tones and harmonic notions. This very disparity was one of the hallmarks of the band's sound: Ellington knew how to pit these voices against one another to gain strong, rich textures of great complexity that, no matter what combination of identifiable musical personalities might be producing them, always somehow sounded Ellingtonian.

Ellington's gifts as a composer are legendary. He was among the greatest of American songwriters, along with the likes of Gershwin, Arlen, and Berlin, and whether or not he was a Delius or a Ravel, he certainly was an elegant and highly capable composer of beautiful, honest program music.

For some years, Ellington downplayed his own abilities as a pianist, but fortunately, he changed his mind. In the 1950s, he began recording in contexts where his playing could be heard prominently and featuring his own work more with the band. His style owes something to his idols James P. Johnson and Willie "The Lion" Smith, and certainly suggests Tatum at times, but his work also carries a hint of Midwestern blues feeling and an angularity that is sometimes reminiscent of Thelonious Monk. He was a very intense pianist, especially in his small-band recordings, and sometimes displayed an almost obsessive denseness of chording. Abandon was not his strong suit. Nevertheless, his was an unusual, attractive style, with plenty of power and great elegance.

Selected Recordings

Big-Band Ellington:

The Beginning (Decca)
The Ellington Era (two volumes, three records each, Columbia)
The Golden Duke (Prestige)
Ellington at Newport (Columbia)
First Time! The Count Meets The Duke (Columbia)
Second Sacred Concert (Fantasy)
Duke Ellington 1938 (Columbia/The Smithsonian Collection)
70th Birthday Concert (Solid State)
New Orleans Suite (Atlantic)
Recollections of the Big Band Era (Atlantic)
The Afro-Eurasian Eclipse (Fantasy)
Eastbourne Performance (RCA)

Small-Band Ellington:

Piano Reflections (Capitol)
Unknown Session (Columbia)
Money Jungle (Solid State)
Duke Ellington and John Coltrane (Impulse)
Duke Ellington Meets Coleman Hawkins (Impulse)
Duke Ellington's Jazz Violin Session (Atlantic)
Duke Ellington—The Pianist (Fantasy)
This One's for Blanton (Pablo)

Miscellaneous:

Duke Ellington/Cincinnati Symphony Orchestra (Decca)
Continuum by the Duke Ellington Orchestra under the direction of Mercer Ellington (Fantasy)

The Decca LP includes the original recording of "Black and Tan Fantasy" and a version of "Yellow Dog Blues" featuring the newly recruited Johnny Hodges. The Columbia *Era* recordings stretch from 1927 to 1940. Each of the two volumes contains three records and the set is an exhaustive representation of Ellington's work throughout that period. Included are first recordings of many Ellington classics, such as "Mood Indigo," "It Don't Mean a Thing (If It Ain't Got That Swing)," "Creole Love Call," and "Reminiscin' in Tempo." A more modest representation of the period is the two-record Columbia/Smithsonian album, which consists of material originally recorded for Brunswick in 1938 and includes relatively few of the better-known Ellington compositions. The Prestige offering is, in fact, big- and small-band Ellington. There are some excellent big-band sides from 1946, when Ray Nance had lately joined the group (he sings a song called "Tulip or Turnip" here), including an Ellington composition called "Happy-Go-Lucky Local," which later became a rhythm-and-blues standard called "Night Train." There is also some two-piano work with Ellington and Strayhorn, accompanied on some tracks only by Wendell Marshall on bass and on others accompanied by bass, drums, and Oscar Pettiford's cello (Strayhorn plays celeste on two of these latter). The Newport recording from the 1956 Newport Jazz Festival, the event at which the Ellington band signalled loud and clear that their doldrums of the early 1950s were over, features Paul Gonsalves's fabled (and seemingly endless) solo on "Dimuendo and Crescendo in Blue." *First Time!* is an amiable meeting between the Ellington and Count Basie orchestras, with both groups playing in full force, side by side. It isn't the best Ellington ever, nor the best Basie, but it is a pleasure indeed to hear such unlikely juxtapositions as Budd Johnson and Paul Gonsalves trading fours or Frank Wess playing flute against Ray Nance's violin. The *Second Sacred Concert* (the first such concert was not recorded), featuring Swedish vocalist Alice Babs and several non-professional choral groups, is sometimes ponderous but contains moments of great orchestral beauty. The Solid State album was recorded in England on Ellington's 1969 European tour (not on his birthday at all). The band is in good form, and some interesting moments are added by organist Wild Bill Davis, who augments the regular crew. Davis appears, too, on *New Orleans Suite;* this is thoughtful, sometimes vaguely melancholy stuff, made all the more so by the fact that Johnny Hodges died halfway through the recording sessions. The big-band–era album is a charming novelty— the Ellington band playing the signature themes of great big bands, from Fletcher Henderson to Jimmie Lunceford to Cab Calloway to Guy Lombardo. The Fantasy LP is a good solid example of Ellington's later programmatic writing, with the reed soloists sounding particularly lively. The RCA disk, recorded live in England late in 1973, is the last official concert recording that Ellington made and includes some rarely heard older Ellington tunes, as well as the haunting "Meditation," the composer's piano showcase from the Second Sacred Concert.

The Capitol small-band LP is piano trio material from 1953, showing Ellington in top form as he plays many of his best-known compositions. *Unknown Session* is a recently discovered 1960 recording by Ellington with a topnotch small band drawn from his regular crew, and including Hodges, Nance, Brown, and Carney. *Money Jungle* is an astonishing piano trio album that was first released on the Douglas label and later re-released at least once by United Artists. It features Charles Mingus and Max Roach and proves that Ellington is capable of understanding bop just as well as he wants to. The Coltrane recording is quartet material, with the saxophonist playing soprano and tenor. One song is by Coltrane, the rest by Ellington and Strayhorn, but the regular rhythm sections of both Coltrane's and Ellington's bands appear in various combinations—Aaron Bell and Sam Woodyard for Ellington, and Jimmy Garrison and Elvin Jones for Coltrane. The two leaders play well together, and the results are suprisingly impressive. The Hawkins LP is more of a piece, with the great tenor saxophonist fitting very comfortably and eloquently into a fine small band made up of Ellington, Hodges, Carney, Nance, Lawrence Brown, Bell, and Woodyard. The violin album offers Ellington (and sometimes Strayhorn), Ray Nance and the great French violinist Stéphane Grappelli on violin, and the Swedish violinist Svend Asmussen, here playing viola. On a little more than half the album, the strings and piano (and rhythm) are joined by Procope, Gonsalves, and trombonist Buster Cooper. It is, in all, elegant stuff. The Fantasy piano album is more piano trio material, this time from 1966 and 1970. The Pablo album echoes duets that Ellington once recorded with bassist Jimmy Blanton, with the bassist here being the superbly confident Ray Brown.

The Cincinnati Symphony Orchestra album (with Erich Kunzel conducting and Ellington as piano soloist) contains three of the longer Ellington compositions, "New World A'Coming," "Harlem" (written in 1950 for Arturo Toscanini's NBC Symphony Orchestra), and "The Golden Broom and the Green Apple," written for the 1965 French-American Festival in New York City. *Continuum* is the Ellington band's first recording under Mercer Ellington's leadership. Much of the personnel has already changed since the last Duke Ellington–led recordings, but the Ellington traditon sounds as if it is in good hands, not only because some earlier Ellington works are here resurrected, but because some of the new, younger soloists seem to have that combination of individualistic voice and Ellingtonian sense that made the band so great for so many years. A guitar has been reintroduced into the band. It is played by Edward Ellington II—Mercer's son, Duke's grandson.

MILES DAVIS *(1926–   )*

The son of a reasonably affluent dentist, Miles Davis was born in Alton, Illinois, and brought up in East St. Louis, Missouri, across the Mississippi from St. Louis. He took up the trumpet on his own and later took lessons from one of his father's patients, a well-known local music teacher. This first formal instruction taught Davis the rudiments of musical theory, but his teacher also introduced him to the work of such fine jazz trumpeters as Harold Baker and Bobby Hackett. According to one story, this teacher is also said to be responsible for Davis's clean, vibrato-less tone, having told the young man, "You're going to get old and start shaking anyway, so don't play vibrato now." Apparently, Davis also met and listened to the St. Louis–born trumpeter Clark Terry during this period. Terry, not much older had developed his fluent, unusual style quite early.

As a teenager, Davis played with a local group called the Blue Devils (no relation to the well-known Walter Page group of the same name. While in the band, he heard Billy Eckstine's bop-era big band when it passed through, and he asked to be allowed to sit in. Nobody was particularly impressed with his playing, but he did make the acquaintance of Charlie Parker and Dizzy Gillespie at that time. Later, while he was still with the Blue Devils, Davis came to the attention of saxophonist Sonny Stitt, who arranged for him to be offered a job touring with drummer/vocalist Tiny Bradshaw's band—an offer that Davis's parents made him refuse.

Juilliard and the Cool

In 1945, his father sent Davis to New York City to study music at Juilliard. (He was later to relate how he spent his first week and his first month's allowance looking for Charlie Parker. He found him.) Davis was a quick study: He attended Juilliard for a time but spent most of his time in the clubs along 52nd Street and elsewhere, listening, sitting in, asking for musical assistance and information. (He is said to have written chord changes down on matchbooks in the darkness of some clubs.) He found work almost at once with Parker, Coleman Hawkins, Benny Carter, and Eddie "Lockjaw" Davis. In November 1945, he made some records with Parker—his first. He joined Parker's regular quintet, and for a short while he was a fixture on 52nd Street. In 1949, however, he struck out on his own for the first time, forming a nine-piece group with an instrumentation previously unknown to jazz: trumpet, trombone,

French horn, alto and baritone saxophones, piano, bass, and drums. This group made only two brief appearances in person, but they did record a classic album on Capitol. Its title, *Birth of the Cool,* was prophetic, because this new music—bop-oriented, but light in texture and more complex, tonally—was largely responsible for the trend towards "cool" jazz that occupied jazz players in the early 1950s.

Between the first two and the last one of the Capitol sessions, Davis appeared at the Paris Jazz Festival with Tadd Dameron and James Moody. When he returned to the United States, he completed the *Cool* recordings, then worked with Milt Jackson and with his own small groups. By this time, Davis had become addicted to heroin. The records made for Blue Note and Prestige during this period are uneven, although at their best, they show Davis for the first time as an original, uncommonly lyrical stylist. By 1954, through sheer strength of character (or simple meanness, some have suggested), Davis had kicked the heroin habit, and his playing became uniformly strong. This was amply demonstrated at the 1955 Newport Jazz Festival, where Davis appeared with his new quintet and played so brilliantly that he became an "overnight"star and was offered a contract by Columbia Records (which he accepted the next year, beginning an association with the company that has lasted until the present day).

Davis and Coltrane

The new Davis quintet was composed of pianist Red Garland, bassist Paul Chambers, drummer Philly Joe Jones, and a remarkable young tenor saxophonist named John Coltrane. (Cannonball Adderly was added on alto saxophone from 1957 to 1959.) This group set the standard for other small bands of the era, becoming one of the most important and most consistently creative small ensembles jazz has ever known. Davis was moving in other directions, too: in 1957, he renewed a professional relationship with composer/arranger/conductor Gil Evans, who had been involved with the *Birth of the Cool* project. Together, they produced an extraordinary big-band album called *Miles Ahead* (the first of several such collaborations), with Davis playing the fluegelhorn—a relative of the cornet with a somewhat meatier tone.

In the early 1960s, Davis formed a new, younger, rather more flamboyant quintet with Herbie Hancock on piano, Ron Carter on bass, Tony Williams on drums, and Wayne Shorter on reeds. After a slow start, this new group grew into a strong, lean, exciting ensemble—as important in its decade as the earlier group had been in the 1950s.

In 1968 and 1969, with this quintet as the basis, Davis made two albums that anticipated, and largely defined, the first stages of rock/jazz fusion music. *Filles de Kilimanjaro,* with Chick Corea and Dave Holland replacing Hancock and Carter on two tracks, tentatively broke down the traditional bop-derived rhythmic structure that even the most advanced avant-garde players of the time still clung to and introduced a heretical element—the electric piano—into serious jazz. *In a Silent Way* was less ambiguous. Here, the personnel included Hancock, Corea, Holland, Shorter, and Williams, in addition to pianist Joe Zawinul and guitarist John McLaughlin. The music was much more (literally) electric, and the rhythmic bases of the music suggested rhythm-and-blues and various kinds of Eastern music more than they suggested bop.

Bitches' Brew

Davis really loosed all restraints for his next album *Bitches' Brew.* Shorter, Corea, McLaughlin, Zawinul, and Holland were still present, but so were a battery of percussionists, a Fender bassist, and a bass clarinetist. The music on the album was, by contemporary standards, indefinable: It certainly wasn't rock, but it didn't sound like anything else in jazz—not even other contemporary jazz/rock experiments. This was a new music, totally Davis's own.

Davis continued to follow his own musical directions into the 1970s. He incorporated Brazilian and Indian percussionists and Indian classical musicians of other types into some of his groups. Then he angled towards rhythm-and-blues, thickening and solidifying the bass lines and incorporating two guitarists into his group. He himself began playing organ and electric keyboard instruments part of the time. Gradually, he even discarded the convention of formal compositions of any kind, however sparse. Instead, he would simply establish a loose rhythmic and harmonic frame for his music, set his musicians to playing, and then lead and direct them, divert them, dissuade them, and kick them in their musical posteriors when they began to lag—his concerts and recording sessions stretch into one or two long, spontaneous collective improvisations apiece. The difference between these sessions and collective improvisations of what might almost be called the conventional avant-garde is that these were directed and shaped by one strong, musically bull-headed leader.

Personal Setbacks

Davis was popular on records and in concerts in the early 1970s, and he toured frequently in the United States and abroad. However, as his music moved more and more toward rhythm-and-blues—at the same time, becoming somehow less accessible, more obtuse—and as he retired his trumpet playing more and more into the background, he lost much of his audience. He had had a serious automobile accident in 1972, and he continuted to be in some pain even after he had supposedly recovered. In 1975, he was hospitalized again, and although he was soon released, he effectively ended his public career—at least for the time being.

The Musical Technician

Davis is a very good trumpeter, one whose technical abilities seem to have grown continuously throughout much of his career; but he is as highly regarded for his content as for his form. His pure, precisely tailored sound became his most noted attribute in the 1950s, but the things that he did with that sound were really what made him so extraordinary a musician. He was, first of all, a superb phraser, an architect of magnificent rhythmic structure. This quality has lasted through all of his work, but first appeared in his ballad playing of the early 1950s, a time when he was one of the finest jazz interpreters of pretty songs such as "It Never Entered My Mind," "Will You Still Be Mine," "Darn That Dream," and "My Old Flame." His work, even on up-tempo numbers and in later years, retained a certain poignancy, an almost poetic delicacy, that was first apparent in these years.

The other thing that first became evident thirty years ago was Davis's ideas about building solo lines. His lines are extremely long—somewhat like a mystery in which the beginning clues make sense only at the end of the story—and he unfolds them in a spare, fragmented, almost teasing manner. His lags, his hesitations, his brief flurries of activity surrounded by silence have the effect of totally engaging the listener, building incredible, quiet tension.

The remarkable thing is that this technique has existed in Davis's music almost since the beginning. On his last albums of the 1970s, behind the electronics and the rhythmic rhetoric, he is still stretching long, elegant lines out against dramatic groundwork, just as he did in the 1950s. (His keyboard playing is another matter. It sounds as if he uses it more as a goad to his musicians than as a solo voice for himself.) Certainly, one aspect of Davis's genius is his recognition that his lines needed a new kind of background, one both hospitable and challenging, and his knowledge of how—and out of what unlikely tools—to build it.

As a composer, Davis has written a number of good, not particularly unusual compositions in various styles at various stages of his career. Some of his most interesting work as a writer—the informal compositions of the early 1970s—can't really be said to have been "written."

The Musical Leader

Davis's chief skill, other than as a trumpeter, is as a leader and mentor of other musicians. In the earlier parts of his career, he gave jobs and inspiration to such players as saxophonists Sonny Rollins, Jackie McLean, and Jimmy Heath. Herbie Hancock had a good commercial reputation when Davis hired him but wasn't yet taken very seriously as a musician, and neither John Coltrane nor Wayne Shorter was particularly well-known until their stays with Davis. A great many of the musicians who were to become prominent in fusion and other recent varieties of jazz put in apprenticeships with Davis: Zawinul, McLaughlin, Corea, and Williams; Hancock and Shorter; drummers Jack DeJohnette, Billy Cobham, and Lenny White; keyboard players Keith Jarrett and Larry Young; saxophonists Bennie Maupin, Gary Bartz, Steve Grossman, Carlos Garnett, and Sonny Fortune; bassist Michael Henderson; and many others. Those who have worked with Davis say that he is extremely demanding, extracting degrees of energy and imagination from musicians that even they didn't know they had. Virtually every musician who has worked for Davis in recent years has come away from the group playing better, more adventuresomely, more confidently. Considering who some of these musicians are, and what they have contributed to contemporary music, this fact alone is enough to earn Davis a place in the jazz pantheon.

Selected Recordings

Birth of the Cool (Capitol)
Miles Davis (United Artists)
Collectors' Items (Prestige)
The Beginning (Prestige)
Workin' (Prestige)
Facets (CBS/France)
Miles Ahead (Columbia)
Sketches of Spain (Columbia)
Seven Steps to Heaven (Columbia)
Miles Smiles (Columbia)
Filles de Kilimanjaro (Columbia)
In a Silent Way (Columbia)
Bitches' Brew (Columbia)
Miles at the Fillmore (Columbia)
Get Up With It (Columbia)
Agharta (Columbia)

The fabled Capitol nonet recordings have been reissued on that label several times—most recently, with the addition of a vocal track, "Darn That Dream," featuring Kenny Hagood. The United Artists album is a two-record set of Blue Note reissues from 1952–54 that features Davis in quartet and sextet contexts with horn players Jackie McLean or Jimmy Heath and trombonist J. J. Johnson. The first Prestige LP includes takes from two sessions—the first (1953) with Sonny Rollins and Charlie Parker (on tenor saxophone), the second (1956) with Rollins and pianist Tommy Flanagan, and including two good Davis blues compositions. The second Prestige is a quartet date with Red Garland and Philly Joe Jones, and the redoubtable Oscar Pettiford on bass. It was recorded in 1955, several months before Davis's "comeback" at Newport. *Workin'* may well be the best of the six or seven recordings made by the Coltrane quintet of the 1950s. The French CBS disk is a compilation of intriguingly disparate elements from 1958 through 1962—two tracks by the Coltrane quintet, two tracks with vocalist Bob Dorough (singing, in one instance, the bitterly funny "Blue Xmas"), four tracks from a big-band date arranged and conducted by the French composer/pianist Michel Legrand, and two tracks with The Brass Ensemble of the Jazz and Classical Music Society, conducted by Gunther Schuller. The first two Columbia LPs are big-band sessions led by Gil Evans—both of them jazz classics. The second of the two is largely devoted to an interpretation of Joaquin Rodrigo's "Concierto de Aranjuez." *Seven*

Steps shows Davis pushing his old quintet into a looser, more emotional stance than that taken in the past. *Miles Smiles* is one of the strongest of the Shorter/Hancock quintet dates. The next three albums, which have already been discussed, are seminal works for the directions that jazz has followed in the 1970s. The Fillmore album, recorded live at the popular San Francisco rock concert hall, is an extension of ideas proposed in *Bitches' Brew* and is particularly notable for guitarist John McLaughlin's work. *Get Up With It* is dedicated to Duke Ellington yet has a stronger rhythm-and-blues feeling than any of Davis's previous records: there are two, and sometimes three, guitars on some tracks, and Davis plays keyboards frequently— on one track, setting aside his trumpet altogether. The final LP was apparently Davis's last recording (excluding re-releases of older material). It was taped live in Japan in 1975 and features music that is somewhat less cluttered than that which his previous few albums had offered. It is tremendously stirring, driving stuff, although Davis's lines here are broken up almost to the point of incoherence.

–8–
Foreign Parts

There are those who say that jazz has an embarrassing little secret—that, despite its American (and ultimately African) origins, it is based largely on European musical traditions, and thus is really not at all the indigenous American (or Afro-American) art form it is so often claimed to be. Those who hold this opinion point out that most jazz is vitally dependent upon Western harmonic, and often rhythmic, ideas. (Even when New Orleans was producing the first great jazz musicians, literacy in conventional or European music was widespread.) In addition, they note that, with the exception of drums, virtually all the important instruments of jazz—saxophone, trumpet, trombone, bass, guitar, even synthesizer—are European in provenance. Jazz and "classical" elements have frequently been fused with apparent facility and at least moderate success (by Paul Whiteman, Duke Ellington, Miles Davis, John Lewis, Stan Kenton, and Gil Evans, among others), and suggesting more than a casual kinship between the two kinds of music.

However, there are those who say that this is nonsense—that jazz is not only American, but specifically black American, a musical expression of black feeling. They believe that attempts to give it European patrimony are not only inaccurate, but also dishonest and racist.

However, despite disagreement about the roots of and influences on jazz, there is little doubt about the other end of the flow, about where jazz has *gone:* it has gone everywhere. Whether or not jazz is of European derivation to begin with, it cannot be denied that it has been welcomed there and that Europe has proven a most prolific source of jazz musicians.

The Beginnings

Ragtime reached Paris and London before the First World War, gaining some popularity as a part of music hall and cabaret entertainments. After the war, several bands drawn from black American army orchestras (one of them led by the appropriately named pianist/violinist James Reese Europe) introduced intimations of jazz, if not the thing itself, to curious and ultimately hospitable European audiences. In 1919, Sidney Bechet went to Europe—where he was to remain for more than two years— with Will Marion Cook's Syncopated Southern Orchestra, and the same year, the Original Dixieland Jass Band embarked on a European tour. (Ironically, most of the black American musicians in Europe in the early 1920s were attached to dance bands or novelty groups, while white jazz players were often able to perform in "purer" jazz contexts.)

By the late 1920s, European popular musicians had assimilated enough jazz ideas from visiting Americans and from the first jazz recordings to reach their countries to be able to start playing the game themselves. By the end of the decade, French musicians like trumpeter Philippe Brun and trombonist Léo Vauchant and British players like Scots trombonist George Chisholm and the Paris-born English saxophonist Buddy Featherstonhaugh had made their debuts as highly competent, if not exactly original, jazz performers.

Swing Influences

Many of the most important American jazz musicians of the era toured Europe in the early 1930s: Louis Armstrong first reached the Continent in 1932, Duke Ellington in 1933, and Coleman Hawkins in 1934. As a result, imitative but often very good European soloists and ensembles became more and more common. By the middle of the decade, Europe had produced her first (and, to this day, greatest) jazz genius—Belgian-born Gypsy guitarist Django Reinhardt, who, as a kind of link between Eddie Lang and Charlie Christian, virtually invented the modern jazz guitar. Reinhardt first achieved recognition in Paris as a member of the Quintet of the Hot Club of France, a jazz appreciation society under the direction of French music critic Hugues Panassié. The other key member of the group was violinist Stéphane Grappelli, a wonderfully inventive musician who has proven to be the most durable of jazz violinists and whose career continues energetically to this day. Later, Reinhardt became associated with a very fine Goodman-influenced French clarinetist named Hubert Rostaing, who also is still active. After Reinhardt, the first European jazz musician to attract serious attention in America was British pianist George Shearing, who plays relatively unadventuresome but very well-crafted swing-derived bop, often utilizing a "locked-hands" chording style developed by the St. Louis swing pianist/organist Milt Buckner and the West Coast pianist/arranger Phil Moore.

American GIs in Europe during and after the Second World War helped to spread interest in jazz there still further, and the growing number of American expatriate jazz musicians who settled in France (most of them) and the Scandinavian countries in the 1950s gave local audiences a chance to hear, and local musicians a chance to play with, serious jazz performers on a regular basis. Battles that had been fought somewhat earlier in the United States about the relative merits of traditional jazz, swing, bop, and everything that preceded them fought again in Europe. When the smoke cleared, it became evident that the bop and post-bop styles were particularly suited to the European temperament. Certainly, there had been good European players of traditional jazz and swing, but now they were vastly outnumbered by musicians who developed strong, often highly original post-Parker vocabularies of their own.

Contemporary European Jazz

Since the mid-1960s, European jazz musicians have been truly important in the worldwide development of jazz for the first time. Performers like the Algerian-born French pianist Martial Solal, the Spanish pianist Tete Montoliu, and the Danish bassist Niels-Henning Ørstead Pederson, for instance, are known for their technical and creative brilliance by jazz fans everywhere. European jazz musicians have frequently outstripped their American counterparts and, in many cases, led the way for them. Much of the important post-Coltrane and post-Coleman "new jazz" and a great deal of the better jazz/rock fusion music of the past fifteen years or so has been created not by Californians or New Yorkers but by musicians from England, France, Scandinavia, and Eastern Europe.

Among the best-known and influential of these musicians are English guitarist John McLaughlin, English saxophonist John Surman (whose technical facility, eclectic style, and highly personal aesthetic sensibility typify the best of the new European jazz), and Hungarian guitarist Attila Zoller (whose style resembles Wes Montgomery's). From Germany came bassist Eberhard Weber (a virtual poet of the Fender bass) and pianist/arranger/composer Claus Ogerman (currently writing and arranging elegant jazz/pop in California). The Czechs produced bassists George Mraz and Miroslav Vitous and pianist Jan Hammer (prominent in the jazz/rock fusion movement). Still more notables are French violinist Jean-Luc Ponty (the heir apparent to Stéphane Grappelli's title as most durable and versatile of the European jazz string players), Norwegian guitarist Terje Rypdal (a musician's musician, who is better known to other guitarists than to the general public), Polish violinist Michal Urbaniak (a leader of his country's academic avant-garde), and Austrian keyboard player Joe Zawinul (founding member of the definitive jazz/rock fusion group, Weather Report).

South American Jazz

Other continents than Europe have also produced fine jazz musicians, of course. Jazz found its way to South America early on, and by the late 1920s, there were a number of jazz-flavored dance bands in Buenos Aires, Caracas, and other capitals.

Argentina has been particularly prolific in producing jazz musicians. The two most famous are pianist/composer Lalo Schifrin and saxophonist Gato Barbieri. Schirin was heard to fine advantage with the Dizzy Gillespie quintet of the early 1960s and has subsequently become an unusually productive TV and film composer in Hollywood. Barbieri played passionately with Don Cherry's group in the mid-1960s, and later became famous for the music he wrote and played for the notorious Bernardo Bertolucci film *Last Tango in Paris.* He then made some fascinating albums blending jazz with traditional South American music of various kinds, and finally turned his talents to a more commercial jazz idiom. Other particularly good Argentinian jazz players include the young swing saxophonist Carlos Hector Acosta (who patterns his groups after the Quintet of the Hot Club of France), mainstream/bop pianist Enrique Villegas and bassist Alfredo Remus, and, in a more modern vein, pianist/composer Alberto Favero, tenor saxophonist Horacio Borraro, and trumpeter Gustavo Bergalli.

Brazil also has produced a large number of fine jazz musicians, but it is something of a special case. The Brazilians, perhaps more than any other group of jazz players outside the United States, have developed their own version of the music. It is strongly grounded not only in American jazz tradition, but also in local Indian and African-influenced percussion music and in the seductive hybrid form of samba. Brazilian jazz, as it might be called, is usually lyrical, lilting music with a rhythmic complexity that is not necessarily apparent to the casual listener. It is also, almost without exception, music you can dance to. Americans know a popular form of Brazilian jazz under the name "bossa nova," but there are other forms of it which are by no means so polite and homogeneous.

Some Brazilian jazz musicians have performed with great skill and authenticity in more conventional jazz contexts: percussionist Airto Moreira has played jazz drums with Chick Corea and percussion with Miles Davis; the composer and classical/jazz guitarist Laurindo Almeida has performed with scores of American jazz stars, including the Modern Jazz Quartet and a group called the L.A. Four; and the lesser-known pianist Fernando Martins and drummer Nelson Serra de Castro have worked extensively in Paris, sometimes with American musicians. Even so, these and others like them remain equally conversant with their native idiom. Other prominent Brazilian jazz musicians, some of whom are known here through their connection with bossa nova, include guitarists Baden Powell, Bola Sete, Luiz Bonfá, and Oscar Castro Neves; trombonist Raul de Souza; saxophonist/singer Moacir Santos; pianists Eumir Deodato and João Donato; flautist Copinha; percussionists Mayuto and NáNá; and multi-instrumentalists Hermeto Pascoal and Sivuca. (Virtually all Brazilian jazz musicians are multi-instrumentalists. It's rare to find a percussionist who doesn't also play at least a bit of guitar or piano, and it's almost impossible to find a Brazilian musician or singer of any kind who doesn't also play percussion.)

Brazil also has a rich tradition of jazz/pop singer/songwriters. While these are not, strictly speaking, jazz musicians or even Brazilian jazz musicians, the lines are sometimes difficult to draw, and almost all of them have had at least some association with pure jazz. The most famous of these, without a doubt, are João Gilberto, Antonio Carlos Jobim, and Sergio Mendes (the latter of whom released one solid Brazilian jazz LP, called *Roots,* in the midst of his pop career).

African Jazz
West Africa has produced a large number of jazz-influenced musicians, many of them saxophonists and percussionists, but few of them have become known outside their own countries (one exception being the fine Nigerian guitarist Fred Coker). South Africa, on the other hand, has exported a score or more of highly skilled jazz players in the past two decades. (Of course, South Africa is among the most Europeanized of African states—the European-influence argument again.) The most famous of these is trumpeter Hugh Masekela. He has had several periods of success as a pop musician in the United States, but made one excellent two-record set of jazz called *Home Is Where the Music Is* in this country in the early 1970s. Other prominent South African jazz musicians, all of whom have had their greatest success in London, are alto saxophonist Dudu Pukwana (who appears on the aforementioned Hugh Masekela LP), pianists Dollar Brand (who also uses the name Abdullah

Ibrahim) and Chris MacGregor, trumpeter Mongezi Feza, and drummer Louis Moholo.

Japanese Jazz

Japan also has produced a number of fine jazz musicians in recent years. Those best-known in the United States are saxophonist Sadao Watanabe, who has worked with Chico Hamilton, Gabor Szabo, and Gary McFarland; guitarist Yoshiaki Masuo, who has played with Lee Konitz, Sonny Rollins, and Elvin Jones, among others; and pianist/composer Toshiko Akiyoshi who has co-led bands with her first husband, saxophonist Charlie Mariano, and her present husband, saxophonist Lew Tabackin.

There are precious few countries that lack good jazz, and there is surely not a one in which jazz has not been heard and loved. Whatever the lineage of jazz may have been, it has grown up to speak a language that everyone can understand.

DJANGO REINHARDT *(Jean-Baptiste Reinhardt) (1910–53)*

Born in the Belgian town of Liverchies into a Gypsy tribe of Northern European origin, Django Reinhardt (the *D* is silent) spent his youth wandering throughout Belgium and France with his family's caravan. He taught himself to play banjo and guitar and seems to have become quite proficient at the latter by the time he was in his midteens. When he was 18, he was badly burned in a fire in the caravan and lost the use of two fingers on his left hand. He began playing the guitar again almost immediately, however, and his accident forced him to play in a purer, more deliberate way and may even have improved his guitar style.

No one knows exactly when Reinhardt first became exposed to jazz, much less when he first tried to play it. It must have been very soon after he injured his hand, because by 1933, in Paris, he had already teamed up with violinist Stéphane Grappelli in a jazz-flavored dance band led by bassist Louis Vole and had joined Vole, Grappelli, and several other guitarists (including his own brother Joseph) in a series of informal jazz jam sessions between regular jobs.

In 1932, some young Parisians had formed a jazz appreciation society, which they dubbed The Hot Club of France. Critics Hugues Panassié and Charles Delaunay were prominent in its leadership and, at the critics' suggestion, the Hot Club began to sponsor jazz concerts for their members and guests. In 1934, they presented one of the Vole/Grappelli/Reinhardt jam sessions to the public, and the group was so enthusiastically received that they stayed on to become the Quintet of the Hot Club of France.

Reinhardt had made his first recordings—non-jazz, playing the banjo—in 1928, and he had appeared on several records with Vole's orchestra, but his first real jazz playing on records came late in 1934, when Panassié arranged for the quintet to cut versions of the traditional classics "Dinah" and "Tiger Rag." The effect of the group on the Paris jazz scene was electric. Their all-string instrumentation (three guitars, bass, and violin) made them seem somehow quintessentially European, but their ability to swing was formidable, and their jazz feeling—especially that of Grappelli and the Reinhardt brothers—was authentic. They played jazz as surely as any of the American musicians who had begun passing through Europe, but they weren't just copying the Americans. They were Europe's own. The Americans were impressed too, especially with Reinhardt, and he performed and recorded with any number of American musicians, including Barney Bigard, Benny Carter, and pioneer jazz violinist Eddie South.

Grappelli left the Hot Club group during the Second World War (although he and Reinhardt were reunited on a number of occasions, including some of the guitarist's last recording sessions). Both the personnel and the instrumentation of the quintet continued to change until it was disbanded in the early 1950s. Reinhardt continued to record with the group, off and on, for the rest of his life (switching from acoustic to electric guitar some time in the mid-1940s), but he also formed a long and successful alliance with Hubert Rostaing, an excellent clarinetist/saxophonist whose pure Goodman-like tone matched Reinhardt's lines perfectly.

In 1946, Reinhardt toured briefly with the Duke Ellington orchestra, and he made his only trip to the United States with that group. His behavior with the band was erratic, though, and his playing was uneven. His health was affected by high blood pressure; he drank heavily; and he would often disappear for days at a time, rejoining a Gypsy caravan briefly if the mood struck him.

In the late 1940s, Reinhardt went into something of a decline, but in 1951, he made a strong comeback at the Club St. Germain in Paris, with alto saxophonist Hubert Fol and pianist Maurice Vander. He continued to play well, if sporadically, for the rest of his life. He died in 1953 of a stroke suffered while fishing.

Reinhardt was a remarkable musician whose style was spare and clean, solid and self-confident and whose harmonic concepts were sophisticated and often strikingly original. He also has a loose, swinging rhythmic sense that lent his music a most attractive warmth, an elegant nonchalance. As a composer, Reinhardt was technically elementary, but he wrote pieces of great melancholic beauty ("Mélodie au crépuscule," the classic

"Nuages"), impressive energy ("Micro [Mike]"), and even boppish good humor ("Place de Broukère," "Black Night").

Reinhardt was one of the most influential musicians that jazz has ever known. The only important jazz guitarist before him was Eddie Lang, the Italian-American from Philadelphia whose recordings with violinist Joe Venuti are among the highest achievements of the swing era. Even including the seminal Charlie Christian, virtually every later jazz guitarist (with the possible exception of some of the less "guitaristic" members of the avant-garde) derives from Lang or Reinhardt—and mostly from the latter, or the former by way of the latter. Reinhardt followed Lang's lead in giving the guitar a horn-like solo ability it had never had before, and he established the linear bases on which almost all jazz guitar improvisation is based today.

Selected Recordings

Django 1934 (GNP)
Django '35–'39 (GNP)
The Versatile Giant (Inner City)
Memorial Django Reinhardt (Vogue)
Django in Rome (EMI/Parlophone)
The Immortal Django Reinhardt (GNP)

The first GNP album includes "Dinah," "Tiger Rag," and the rest of Reinhardt's work from his first year of recording with the Quintet of the Hot Club of France (including "Avalon," "Sweet Sue," and "Confessin' "). Reinhardt sounds fine, but has not yet developed his own style fully. The second GNP record is another story. This is prime-quality material from what is arguably Reinhardt's (and, for that matter, Grappelli's) best period—all with the Hot Club group. Reinhardt sounds fresh and enthusiastic, and he seems often to throw off the fastest, most intricate little runs as if they were afterthoughts. The Inner City LP contains a wide selection of solo and small-group work from 1934–51 and has two tracks that were recorded with Duke Ellington in 1946, "Honeysuckle Rose" and "Improvisations on 'Tiger Rag'." The album on the French Vogue label is a good sampler of post-War material and was mostly taken from French radio transcriptions. It includes tracks with the Hot Club quintet in two different incarnations (one with Grappelli), a solo improvisation, a strange track with a band led by an American named Jack Platt (recorded live at the Salle Pleyel), and one piece from Reinhardt's 1951 appearance at the Club St. Germain. Half of the recordings from Rome come from an album of tracks with Grappelli and a local rhythm section (1949), and half are from sessions with a 1950 version of the Hot Club quintet, featuring André Ekyan. There is some strange material here—a bizarre version of "The Peanut Vendor" and a Reinhardt arrangement of Grieg's "Danse Norvegienne," for example—but Reinhardt plays fast and furiously, showing off his technical abilities especially well. The final GNP album is late Reinhardt, mostly from 1953, including four tracks with a re-vivified version of an early Hot Club quintet (Grappelli, Joseph Reinhardt, Fred Hermelin, and guitarist Eugène Vees) and ten tracks with Hubert Rostaing, including a stunning version of Debussy's "Rêverie" (identified on the LP as a Reinhardt com-position called "Django's Dream").

MARTIAL SOLAL   *(1927–   )*

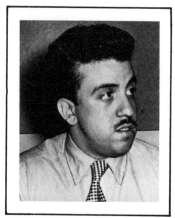

Born in Algiers and a student of the piano since he was 7, Solal heard his first jazz records when he was barely a teenager and de-cided to develop his talents in the direction of that music. In 1950, he moved to Paris and became active in the local jazz scene, per-forming regularly at the Club St. Germain. There he worked with many of the fixtures of the Paris jazz scene at that time, including French trumpeter Roger Guérin, Belgian vibraharpist Fats Sadi, guitarist René Thomas, and ex-patriate American guitarist Jim-my Gourley. His technical abilities were in full flower by this time, and he became popular with American musicians who passed through Paris, playing with notables like Sidney Bechet, Lucky Thompson, Stan Getz, Don Byas, and Kenny Clarke.

In the later 1950s, he turned his attention more toward com-posing. He has written not only innumerable jazz works, many of them extremely complex, but also some thirty or forty film scores and several long, rather serious works, including a suite for oboe, cello, and jazz trio called "Rhythmical Escape." He has worked frequently with a trio (either bass and drums or two basses) but often performs alone—a context for which his agile, orchestral piano style is particularly appropriate. He continues to be active, both as a composer and a pianist and is, by many accounts, the most brilliant pianist playing jazz in Europe today.

Solal's abilities are virtuosic. His sensibility is certainly an academic one (among his compositions is "Ah! Non," a hilar-ious transmogrification of a Hanon piano exercise). One of his partisans, French jazz critic Alain Gerber, argues that his rep-utation for technical brilliance has militated against him, in fact—that "he has been more praised and less listened to than most musicians of his generation"—but he injects a good deal of humor into his playing, and his frequent and often astonish-ing changes of key, tempo, and mood seem emotionally rather than intellectually derived. He can also swing as well as anyone. His methodology involves the statement of themes with the maximum possible measure of embellishment, and then the construction of solos in obtuse, complicated ways, with harmonic relationships turned inside out and rhythmic patterns fragmented in a manner that suggests a streamlined Art Tatum. Solal also has remarkable ability to play one hand against the other at different tempos, and sometimes in different keys

Selected Recordings

Key for Two by the Martial Solal/Hampton Hawes Quartet (BYG)
Martial Solal en Solo (French RCA)
Zoller-Koller-Solal (MPS)
Satori by Lee Konitz (Milestone)
Duplicity by Lee Konitz and Martial Solal (Horo)

The BYG LP features Solal in an unusual two-piano quartet with the late American pianist Hampton Hawes, and bassist Pierre Michelot, and drummer Kenny Clarke. The other pianist's steady, bluesy style holds Solal back sometimes, but it also provides an attractive, dramatically contrasting field for him to play against. The solo record is brilliant, allowing Solal to muse, meander, and jump about at his own pace. Included are several very good compositions of his, among them "Ah! Non" and the impossibly complex counterpoint of "Blues Antagoniste." The MPS album shows Solal in a fairly straightforward, hard-swinging context. The first Konitz disk finds Solal swinging even harder, with a topnotch rhythm team of bassist Dave Holland and drummer Jack DeJohnette behind him. The second Konitz LP, recorded in 1977 for the Italian Horo label, is a two-record set of unaccompanied duets between the alto saxophonist and the pianist, showing Solal in a sparer, freer style than usual.

JOHN SURMAN   *(1944–   )*

Born in the English town of Tavistock, Surman studied music at the London College of Music. He became a part of the fledgling British "new jazz" scene in the early 1960s—mostly playing baritone saxophone, although he also plays soprano saxophone, bass clarinet, piano, and various synthesizers. His first steady job was with Mike Westbrook's medium-big bands of the time, and he also worked with pianist Chris McGregor, guitarist John McLaughlin, and other key London jazz figures throughout the 1960s. In 1969, he formed a group called the Trio, with drummer Stu Martin and bassist Barre Phillips. He felt constrained by the trio format, however, and started showing signs that he was tired of performing. He retired until 1973, then returned to a career of recording and performing, both as a leader and as a part of other musicians' bands. He continues to be active.

England has produced more than her share of excellent saxophonists in recent decades, including many younger players who play what might be described as a sort of well-behaved avant-garde—respectful of earlier traditions but not bound by them. Of these saxophonists, Surman is probably the best. He has a mature, almost old-fashioned tone, particularly on baritone saxophone, and his breathing is very even, his attack very firm. He is a perfect saxophonist for big bands, with which he often plays: his rich, controlled sound adds strength and character to ensemble playing, but he also has the power and the edge of sharpness necessary to sing out from the band in solo passages. There is obviously a good deal of John Coltrane in his playing, but there are also elements of that hard-swinging, post-bop, pre-Coltrane warmth found in saxophonists like Booker Ervin and Charles Davis. He is, in any case, extremely eloquent and full of emotional vitality, and he is nearly always exciting to hear.

Selected Recordings

Anglo-Sax (Deram)
Tales of the Algonquin by John Surman and John Warren (Deram)
Westering Home (Help)
The Trio (Pye)
Upon Reflection (ECM)

The first Deram album is, for some inexplicable reason, subtitled "Jazz Alto." In fact, one side does feature a sextet including Mike Osborne on alto saxophone, but the other side (from 1969) is by an eleven-piece ensemble (including trumpeters Harry Beckett and Kenny Wheeler and bassist Dave Holland), and Surman plays baritone saxophone throughout. The second Deram disk is an ambitious big- band LP written and arranged by another good English baritone saxophonist, John Warren. Wheeler and Beckett are here, too, and the rest of the reed section is Mike Osborne, Stan Sulzmann, and Alan Skidmore, notables all. The Help album is a vaguely "free," vaguely programmatic series of pieces composed and played entirely by Surman, who overdubs piano, synthesizer, and other reed instruments with his baritone saxophone. The trio recording is with Phillips and Martin and is particularly interesting for the way in which the three musicians follow each other, phrase for phrase, in some sequences, goading each other along. The EMC recording, from 1979, is another solo album, but it is much different from *Westering Home*—quieter, more lyrical, more dependent on electronics, and even vaguely hypnotic.

—9—
The
New Thing

Jazz of any kind is somewhat of a new thing to the world of music. By anyone's reckoning, it is less than 100 years old, and it hasn't been heard widely for much more than half a century. What the pioneer jazz players of New Orleans and the Midwest were doing in their early days might have been rather tame stuff by contemporary classical standards (Louis Armstrong was only 11 when Arnold Schoenberg wrote his "Pierrot Lunaire"), but it was positively revolutionary in American popular music, and its theoretical bases (or perhaps its refreshing lack of them) were thought scandalous by the academicians.

In its own way, jazz was a manifestation (unconsciously, of course) of the overall musical avant-garde—one that was ultimately far more influential on concert music than either jazz or classical musicians could possibly have foreseen. It was also, by its very nature (highly personal, intuitive, ungrounded in homogeneous tradition), a kind of music that tended to re-invent itself continually, to spawn new avant-gardes within the context of itself: by the standards set in New Orleans and Chicago, there was something vaguely revolutionary about swing; bop was dramatically revolutionary by any previous standards; and the more European-derived cool jazz was a fast break with bop.

Tradition vs the Avant Garde

Nevertheless, all these kinds of jazz, and other sub-groups that were played contemporaneously with them, existed within certain apparently implicit rules: a small number of basic song forms was utilized; bar lines and time signatures knew their place (even if they didn't always keep to it); and the bases of improvisation were harmonic. The first true avant-garde in jazz changed the rules. Hinted at by Lennie Tristano and Lee Konitz as early as 1949 and brought into flower in the late 1950s by saxophonist Ornette Coleman, trumpeter Don Cherry, pianist Cecil Taylor (working from a different direction), and their associates, the avant-garde expanded the jazz form, broke the old covenants, accepted atonality and unconventional modes ("new" old ways of casting the scale), and was more likely to base improvisations on emotional impulses or random spiritual inspirations than on the old familiar building blocks of chords.

The avant-garde—"free jazz," "new music," "the new thing"—was by far the sharpest and seemingly irreparable turn away from what had come before that jazz had ever taken: there were those who thought that jazz would die because of it. Taylor and, especially, Coleman and Cherry were fiercely controversial; Coleman, specifically, was frequently denounced as a charlatan and once, in his early days, was even beaten up by some men who were incensed at the way he played.

Coleman and Cherry met in Los Angeles in the late 1950s and found that they had musical ideas in common. They worked for a time in a group led by pianist Paul Bley, a meticulous craftsman who was quietly breaking out of harmonic improvisation himself, and were later championed by bassists Red Mitchell and Percy Heath, who encouraged them to record with their own group. Their first several albums sent shock waves throughout the jazz community, winning them both enmity and vibrant praise—the latter, from people like pianist John Lewis, composer Gunther Schuller, and several of the more important New York–based jazz critics. More important, though, was the fact that their records and personal appearances seemed to act as a catalyst on other musicians who had been leaning away from the way jazz was being played at the time. Coleman and Cherry opened doors, and before long, there were scores of other players pouring through. By the time the two musicians recorded their landmark album *Free Jazz* in 1960, there was already a small but thriving avant-garde jazz scene in New York.

The Revolutionary Anthem

Free Jazz was a 36½-minute, uninterrupted, improvised anthem for the avant-garde, featuring two complete quartets playing polyphonically against each other (stereo channel to stereo channel, rather than nave to nave). Coleman played the white plastic alto saxophone that was to become his trademark for some years, and Cherry used a compact "pocket trumpet" that he has often favored since. Each of the other musicians also had something special to offer. The remarkable one of these, Eric Dolphy, was the most lyrical and most "classical" and harmonically-oriented of the avant-garde reed players. Here, he uses only bass clarinet, the instrument from his arsenal of woodwinds that he seemed to favor most. Trumpeter Freddie Hubbard, an intense, post–Miles Davis player with a beautiful rich tone, performs here with fire and imagination but never really plays "free." Also notable are brilliant bassist Scott LaFaro, who was on the cusp of the avant-garde but also plays somewhat conservatively in this company, and Charlie Haden, perhaps the purest, firmest of the new bassists of the period. One of the drummers was Billy Higgins, a crisp, agile player who had worked successfully in numerous cool and hard jazz bands and who was on Coleman's and Cherry's first LP under their own names in 1959. The other was Ed Blackwell, a New Orleans–born musician whose traditionalist background imparts to his playing an orderliness and musicality rare in other modern drummers. Ironically, about a year after this definitive album was released, Coleman chose to retire from public life for several years. Despite this, the avant-garde flourished.

The other important pioneer of the avant-garde in jazz was Cecil Taylor, an energetic, feverishly imaginative pianist who was drawn to the European atonal writing of the early 20th century. He had made his first long-playing record in 1955 with soprano saxophonist Steve Lacy, bassist Buell Neidlinger, and drummer Dennis Charles. It was a far more conventional work than Coleman's and Cherry's first albums were to be, but it was characterized by some of the mutations of tempo and harmony that Coleman had employed, particularly in the piano parts. Taylor's next album, recorded in 1959 with tenor saxophonist Bill Barron and trumpeter Ted Curson, was more out of the ordinary, with Taylor's playing becoming more concentrated and more unorthodox in its phrasing. He was by this time clearly an independent thinker with his own ideas about the new jazz. Taylor and his colleagues approached their music rather formally, basing it on their knowledge of the experiments of academe, while Coleman and Cherry approached jazz more sensually and impressionistically, as a kind of skewed reading of hard bop rather than as an application to jazz of formal (though heretical) principles. Taylor has since moved increasingly away from the academic camp.

Black and Political

For the most part, the new music was Black. There were some extremely fine white musicians involved in key roles in the avant-garde, to be sure—among them, Haden, Neidlinger, LaFaro, bassists Gary Peacock and David Izenzon (who came on the scene slightly later), Lacy, Bley, and trombonist Roswell Rudd (perhaps the finest avant-garde musician on the instrument, with the possible exception of a young player named George Lewis). However, the temperament and guiding energy of the movement, its militancy, were emphatically not white. One spokesman for the music was author/dramatist LeRoi Jones, now called Imamu Baraka, who once wrote, "The expression and instinctive (natural) reflection that characterizes black art and culture ... transcends any emotional state (human realization) the white man knows and "New Black Music is this: Find the self, then kill it."

The basic idea of this was that the new music was, by definition, a statement of black feelings; that white players could reproduce it or augment it but could never honestly create it. A common theme among black musicians in this area was that there was no distance, no difference, between what they played and what they were—that their life and their art informed each other, *were* each other. This implies that they were rejecting not only white social and emotional values, but European-derived musical concepts as well. To what extent even the freest, angriest black jazz successfully eluded basic European forms is a matter for the musicologists to worry.

Jazz had become both political and highly emotional. The effect on much of the new jazz, of such an electrifying outpouring of raw feeling was profound: emotions—especially anger—had rarely, if ever, been so nakedly displayed in jazz before. Much of the music is difficult to listen to both because it demands a particular attention from the listener and because it is sometimes almost unbearably intense and even cacophonic. The best of it is unfailingly stirring, and many of the more impressive players of the idiom have turned out to be superbly durable, contributing much energy, originality, and sheer musical excellence to the jazz tradition—a fact that, in most cases, has become more readily apparent as they have freed themselves from the exigencies of rhetoric.

The Musicians

Among the most influential of these musicians are four reed players—Eric Dolphy, Archie Shepp, Albert Ayler, and Pharoah Sanders. Dolphy was one of the most lyrical, "classical," and harmonically oriented of the major figures of the avant-garde. He was a fine alto saxophonist, but was best known for his work on bass clarinet and flute. He died after a fairly brief career, but not before he had made powerful and eloquent contributions to some of the key albums of the period.

Shepp is a particularly exciting tenor saxophonist, with strong references to Coleman Hawkins and Ben Webster in his tone. He has been a strong, fluent soloist for nearly a generation, frequently filling his works with overt political commentary and/or strong doses of ironic humor—not to mention an obvious affection for rhythm-and-blues that surfaces in the most unlikely places.

Ayler also played with Cecil Taylor for a time but worked mostly with the iconoclastic drummer Sonny Murray and with his own brother, trumpeter Don Ayler. He died tragically and mysteriously in 1970 and clearly never fulfilled his great promise. He had a sinuous, glassy sound that stood out dramatically from that of other saxophonists (he played soprano, alto and primarily, tenor saxophones). More importantly, he had a completely eccentric, eclectic vocabulary of musical notions that he would rush into his solos with such speed and confidence that there was no point questioning them or trying to sort them out. One could only listen. He was perhaps the single most maligned soloist in the New York avant-garde (even many of the other free players didn't like the way he played), but his contributions to that musical form stand up as among the most brilliant and original.

Sanders was perhaps the most relentlessly dynamic of the three—at least in the 1960s, when he blew vast showers of notes, full of overtones and dancing recklessly from lower to upper register, with Don Cherry, John Coltrane, then Coltrane's widow Alice (who plays piano and harp), and his own groups. He has mostly played tenor saxophone, and his sound on the instrument is medium-rich and betrays an agility that sometimes leads him into too many changes of direction. In the late 1960s and early 1970s, his concerns with pan-Africanism and religious mysticism began to lend an increasing exotic sound to his music, to the extent that he eventually threatened to become what one writer has called "the Martin Denny of jazz." More recently, he has returned to more straightforward playing.

Coltrane

The other vitally important early figure in the avant-garde in jazz, with Coleman and Taylor, was soprano and tenor saxophonist John Coltrane, considered by many to be the greatest of the three, and certainly the most popular of them. Unlike the other two, Coltrane was already well-established in jazz in more conventional styles (largely through his work with the Miles Davis group) when he began to make his breakthroughs. Further, although he moved into his free jazz period some years after Coleman and Taylor had appeared on the scene, he was not noticeably influenced by them. (Saxophonists like Shepp, Sanders, and Dolphy surely were a kind of inspiration for him, even though he had taught them much of what they knew).

Coltrane was to become perhaps the most influential single jazz musician of the past twenty years, inspiring scores upon scores of other players, saxophonists and otherwise. Among the most notable of these are reed players Gato Barbieri, Joe Farrell (a particularly dramatic, fluid soloist), Wayne Shorter (a wonderfully lyrical player who also shows strongly the influence of Miles Davis, with whom he was long associated), and Dewey Redman (a tough, muscular-sounding saxophonist who has worked frequently with Ornette Coleman). Others are Bennie Maupin (whose warm, burred tone on tenor earns him a place in jazz as the premier bass clarinetist in jazz since Eric Dolphy's death), Carlos Garnett (a raunchy, fiery-sounding tenor saxophonist), and—perhaps most notably of all—Joe Henderson, whose well-rounded, supremely confident amalgamations of avant-garde, hard bop, and mainstream influences make him the most consistently original, continually *interesting* tenor saxophonist of the lot. Not all of these players have worked with any regularity in avant-garde terrain, but all of them have been shaped and emboldened by the new music.

Sun Ra

In a class by himself is Sun Ra (born Herman Blount), a keyboard player who worked in Chicago in the 1950s and became prominent in that city's avant-garde jazz scene before moving, in the early 1960s, to New York. Since his Chicago days, he has led a ten- to seventeen-piece group known variously as the Solar Arkestra, the Myth-Science Arkestra, and the Intergalactic Research Arkestra, which might be described as a kind of left-wing Duke Ellington Band. This last is a highly professional ensemble with a number of strong soloists and its own unique tonal colorations. It plays an individualistic pastiche of jazz, African and miscellaneous Eastern music, and electronics presented with the trappings of astrology and science fiction and staged with the help of energetic theatrics (costumes, dancers, and film shows, for example). The core of Sun Ra's reed section—Marshall Allen, John Gilmore, and Pat Patrick, whose principal instruments are alto, tenor, and baritone saxophones, respectively—is justly famous, and the three men have been with the Arkestra for about a quarter of a century. (Gilmore has recorded widely outside the group as well.) Alan Silva, trombonist Julian Priester, drummer Lex Humphries, and numerous fine, lesser-known performers have also played with Sun Ra. The leader himself is a solid, surprisingly traditional pianist, with stride roots showing. He is outside the main ranks of the avant-garde, but the originality and the stylistic freedom of his work have been a constant inspiration to the new music, and many of its more important practitioners cite him as a major influence.

Chicago and the Avant Garde

Traditionally, certain cities have been considered to have a hallowed place in jazz history. Chicago, of course, is one. It was the second great jazz capital, and many of the best, most influential players of the swing era and after were born and/or brought up there. At least until the Second World War, it was as important a venue for jazz as New York was, if not more so. The city's indigenous bop population is legendary in jazz circles—not just the well-known figures like tenor saxophonist Eddie Harris, but the underservedly obscure as well. It is hardly surprising, then, that Chicago turned out to produce an especially strong, imaginative jazz avant-garde.

One of the key figures in the movement was pianist Muhal Richard Abrams, long known as one of the best session pianists in the city. In 1961, he founded the adventuresome large-scale Experimental Band and, in 1965, organized the Association for the Advancement of Creative Music—which has continued to this day to be the focal point of the new music in Chicago and a wellspring of inspiration for like-minded musicians throughout the Midwest and East. (Oliver Lake's Black Artist Group was one organization that drew direction and encouragement from the AACM.) A number of fine musicians came from Abrams's orbit. Violinist Leroy Jenkins, a formidable musician, has worked with virtually every important figure in the New York avant-garde and now has his own group, the Revolutionary Ensemble, with bassist Sirone and drummer Jerome Cooper. Reed player Anthony Braxton has recorded several long, highly emotional solo albums on alto saxophone and has worked frequently with important members of the European avant-garde, including Kenny Wheeler and Derek Bailey. Others are saxophonists Kalaparusha (Maurice McIntyre) and Fred Anderson, trombonist Lester Lashley, drummers Steve McCall and Thurman Baker, and, most significantly of all, the Art Ensemble of Chicago, a spectacular, relentlessly exciting quartet made up of trumpeter Lester Bowie, saxophonists Joseph Jarman and Roscoe Mitchell, and bassist Malachi Favors—all protean multi-instrumentalists—whose every concert is a vivid, exquisitely played encyclopedia of jazz history.

Recent Developments
The exciting, angry, liberated jazz avant-garde had quieted down somewhat by the late 1970s. All-out "free" playing is heard rather seldom in the United States today (although it still exists in Europe), and most of the major figures of the new music have died (Coltrane, Dolphy, Ayler) or moderated their styles. Many of the younger, more experimental jazz musicians today are animated by electronic circuitry and/or some manifestation of the new spirituality as much as by ethnic politics.

Of course, individualists like Cecil Taylor, Sun Ra, Leroy Jenkins, Sam Rivers, Andrew Hill, Ken McIntyre, Oliver Lake, and others continue to pursue their elusive and demanding muse with as much integrity and originality as ever. Other players have had changes of philosophical heart and now strive to make their music accessible to larger audiences, although—at least theoretically—they would maintain the purity of creative impulse.

What has happened to the jazz avant-garde in general is that it has become less dramatically separate from the rest of jazz. Nevertheless, the heart of the avant-garde—its freedom from the strictures of harmonic improvisation, new tonal and dynamic qualities, rhythmic idiosyncracies, and intensity of emotion—continues to throb brightly. It is now part of the body of jazz.

ORNETTE COLEMAN *(1930–   )*

The Fort Worth–born Coleman taught himself to play alto and tenor saxophones as a teenager, inspired by a saxophonist cousin named James Jordan and by a noted local player named Red Connors. His early musical career is hardly an inspired one. He took a succession of theatre band and rhythm-and-blues jobs and was fired from most of them, apparently, for not being good enough. He got as far as Los Angeles with the rhythm-and-blues band of guitarist/vocalist Pee-Wee Crayton in the mid-1950s and decided to settle there. He worked day jobs while teaching himself musical theory and practicing, and he began to develop his (at that time) strange, atonal style. He was not well liked by other musicians, though he did meet one musician, who understood the way he was beginning to play. This was trumpeter Don Cherry, who, unlike Coleman, had been trained formally in music and had played successfully with conventional local jazz groups. The two joined forces, and each one's playing came to resemble the other's.

Coleman and Cherry refined their music in their own jam sessions, held in a Los Angeles garage. (One of the other musicians who took part was trumpeter Bobby Bradford.) In 1958, both men joined a quintet led by pianist Paul Bley that also featured bassist Charlie Haden and drummer Billy Higgins. Somewhere around this time, the prominent West Coast bassist Red Mitchell heard Coleman and Cherry (the latter of whom had worked with Mitchell at an earlier time) and arranged for them to record for the Los Angeles–based Contemporary label. Their first album, cut in 1959, included pianist Walter Norris, drummer Higgins, and another local bassist, Don Payne. Their second album for the label was piano-less and included Mitchell and drummer Shelley Manne.

Their next great champion was bassist Percy Heath, who admitted that he didn't quite understand what they were getting at but was excited by what he heard. Heath brought them to the attention of his colleague in the Modern Jazz Quartet, pianist John Lewis. Lewis had them invited to a jazz summer school then being held at the Music Inn in Lenox, Massachu-

setts. There they attracted more patrons (and detractors), were hired for their first New York performances, at the Five Spot, and signed a new contract with Atlantic Records.

Their first two Atlantic Recordings, the prophetically named *The Shape of Jazz To Come* and *Change of the Century,* made with (for the first time) a completely sympathetic rhythm section—Charlie Haden and Billy Higgins—announced their arrival on the jazz scene loudly and dramatically. Its release became the first real cause célèbre in jazz since the birth of bop. Famous musicians and well-known critics took sides; *Esquire* magazine devoted an entire article to the question of Coleman's sincerity and importance.

Coleman continued to record and perform, mostly with Cherry (including one album on which he played tenor rather than his usual alto saxophone) until 1962. Then, partly because he couldn't get paid what he thought he was worth as a performer and partly (apparently) because he wanted to rethink some of his music, he retired from public musical life for several years. Coleman's main instrument has always been alto saxophone, but during this period, he taught himself to play violin and trumpet—although in a distinctly unorthodox fashion—and he later recorded an album as a trumpeter in hard-bop alto saxophonist Jackie McLean's quintet. At the same time, he invited other musicians to play informally with him in his New York loft.

In 1965, Coleman burst upon the jazz scene again with a trio including bassist David Izenzon and drummer Donald Moffett, both of whom had worked briefly with him before his retirement. (The group was sometimes augmented with a second bassist, Charlie Haden.)

In the late 1960s, Coleman worked with a trio that included Charlie Haden and his own son Ornette Denardo, then brought in another reed player, Dewey Redman, with whom he continued to be associated for some years. He was to make several albums with Redman and John Coltrane's one-time rhythm section of Jimmy Garrison on bass and Elvin Jones—with whom he and Cherry had recorded in the early 1960s—on drums. Coleman also began writing longer, formal works, performing them with the Philadelphia Woodwind Quintet and other chamber groups. He developed his compositional theories into a concept he calls "harmolodic," which, he says, "means that the rhythms, harmonies and tempos are all equal in relationship and independent melodies at the same time." He dropped from sight again for several years in the mid-1970s, and then resurfaced with a group consisting of two guitarists, an electric bassist, and a drummer—none of them known in jazz circles. Since then, he has been working in a style that owes much to rhythm-and-blues and to the minimalist compositions of Phillip Glass, Steve Reich, and Terry Riley, among others.

Coleman was probably the single most important figure in the jazz avant-garde in its first decade or so. John Coltrane made his immense contributions to the music more cautiously and conventionally, and thus less dramatically; Cecil Taylor is more intellectual, more complex, and hence not as accessible, not as overtly influential. One of the great secrets of Coleman's eventual popularity, as more than one observer has suggested, lies in the fact that he has always been, at heart, a bluesy, hard-rocking, old-fashioned horn man, with much in common with the Texas saxophone tradition. Coleman has also been called the first original jazz saxophonist since Charlie Parker—a large claim, but one not without substance. It is certainly safe to say that, like Parker, he played things that no one had ever heard before. His flashy, warm, extremely human-sounding tone was riveting. He had a way of clanking up against the outsides of the chord changes (many of his classic compositions, like "Lonely Woman," "Ramblin'," "Tears Inside," and "Una Muy Bonita," are in fact wonderful little variations on standard bop and pop song structures); then he would veer off from them altogether. It was often nothing less than thrilling—a fact sometimes forgotten in this age when even studio musicians play "free" solos on Motown singles and television commercials.

Selected Recordings

The Fabulous Paul Bley Quintet (America)
The Shape of Jazz to Come (Atlantic)
Change of the Century (Atlantic)
Free Jazz (Atlantic)
Ornette Coleman in Europe Volume 1 (Polydor/Freedom)
The Ornette Coleman Trio at the "Golden Circle" Stockholm (Blue Note)
Crisis (Impulse)
Science Fiction (Columbia)
Dancing in Your Head (A&M/Horizon)

The Bley album, on the French-based America label, is Coleman, Cherry, Bley, Haden, and Higgins, recorded live (with Bley, unfortunately, not very audible) in 1958 in Los Angeles. Largely due to the rhythm section, this record is better early Coleman than his first two official albums on the Contemporary label, *Something Else!!!!* and *Tomorrow is the Question.* The first two Atlantic albums are definitive early Coleman/ Cherry. The former contains "Lonely Woman" and the latter, "Ramblin'," "Una Muy Bonita," and a Parkerish tune called "Bird Food." The two horns build their solos in much the same ways, but their differences in timbre leave plenty of room for sparks to fly between them. The classic *Free Jazz* on which the one long take is "written" only to the extent of containing introductory themes for each soloist, is intense and often jagged, and, surprise of surprises, it actually *swings* much of the time. The Polydor/Freedom LP and the first Blue Note are both live recordings from 1965. The first was recorded in London and includes one of Coleman's longer works, "Sounds and Forms for Wind Quintet" (with the composer playing trumpet), and two trio tracks with Izezon and Moffett. The second, from a well-known jazz club in Stockholm, features the same trio. (Second volumes exist for both sets, and both include some of Coleman's first recordings on violin.) The Impulse album, recorded live in New York City in 1969, has Coleman on alto saxophone and violin, Don Cherry on trumpet and flute (in his first appearance with Coleman since 1962), Dewey Redman on tenor saxophone and clarinet, Charlie Haden on bass, and Coleman's son on drums. One track, "Space Jungle," with violin, clarinet, and the flute voicing the theme, is particularly beautiful. The Columbia LP is a compilation of tracks, recorded in 1974: two with the old Cherry/Haden/Higgins group; two with Redman, Haden, Higgins, and Ed Blackwell, two trumpeters, and Indian vocalist Asha Puthli; two with Redman, Blackwell, Haden, and trumpeter Bobby Bradford; one with Redman, Cherry, Bradford, Haden, Blackwell, Higgins, and poet David Henderson (reading a work called "Science Fiction"); and one with Haden and Blackwell, Redman playing tenor saxophone and Musette, and Coleman playing violin and trumpet (he otherwise plays alto saxophone here). The album was produced by James Jordan—Coleman's saxophonist cousin from Texas, who was his first inspiration. The A&M/Horizon album offers Coleman playing alto saxophone only—first with his two-guitar quintet, performing two variations on a theme from his symphony, "Skies of America," and then, with clarinetist Robert Palmer, playing against a track featuring the "master musicians of Joujouka, Morocco."

CECIL TAYLOR   *(1933–)*

Born into a Long Island family that included several professional musicians, Taylor was exposed to both classical music and jazz from childhood. He studied piano and musical theory formally—first with private teachers, and later at New York College of Music and the New England Conservatory of Music in Boston. While at the latter institution, he became acquainted with Boston-based jazz musicians like saxophonists Sam Rivers, Gigi Gryce, and Charlie Mariano, trumpeter Joe Gordon, and pianist Jaki Byard, and he soon made a name for himself in their midst as an unusual and technically skilled performer. Returning to New York, he worked with more traditional musicians, including Johnny Hodges and even Hot Lips Page, but by the mid-1950s, he had begun to establish his own style and was moving farther and farther away from conventional jazz.

In 1955, he formed his first regular group, a quartet, with soprano saxophonist Steve Lacy, bassist Buell Neidlinger, and drummer Dennis Charles. Late that year, he recorded his first album, for the Boston-based Transition label. In 1958, vibraharpist Earl Griffith replaced Lacy, and was in turn replaced by tenor saxophonist Archie Shepp.

In 1962, Taylor disbanded the group and began working informally with some of the more prominent members on the New York avant-garde jazz scene, including Roswell Rudd, Albert Ayler, Sonny Murray, and an eclectic alto saxophonist named Jimmy Lyons. He was, by this time, widely recognized as a major figure in the new jazz—*the* major pianist, in fact—and much of his playing was firmly in the "free" style.

In the mid-1960s, Taylor recorded a sextet and a septet album for Blue Note, both of which featured two bassists (Henry Grimes and Alan Silva), but since that time, he has rarely used even one. The unit that he has most often performed and recorded with since 1968 has included Jimmy Lyons and drummer Andrew Cyrille, sometimes augmented by his old comrade from Boston, Sam Rivers. In recent years, he has also appeared frequently as a solo pianist—a context particularly suited to his immense, percussive piano sound and his highly rhythmic orchestral approach to the instrument.

Taylor is particularly remarkable because of the universality of his piano language. He has a far better theoretical background than the vast majority of jazz musicians, and, unlike some others who have formal musical training, he has never rejected what he learned as being superfluous to the jazz experience. His technical skills are admirable. He has a firm, bright, articulate tone and a sophisticated sense of dynamics. Most of all, he has a superb concept of space, of placement of notes. At the same time, he is a moving, highly personal player with an emphatic blues sense that might almost be called "funky" and a raw, gutsy power to his lines. He recalls Horace Silver, Monk, Jaki Byard, sometimes Cage, sometimes Bartók. He is often, especially in his later playing, almost unbearably intense.

Selected Recordings

In Transition (two-record set, Blue Note)
New York City R&B (Barnaby)
Live at the Café Montmartre (Fantasy)
Unit Structures (Blue Note)
Indent (Unit Core)
Silent Tongues (Arista/Freedom)

The first Blue Note set is a two-record reissue containing the complete Transition LP from 1955 (Taylor's debut as a leader) and a United Artists album originally issued under the title *Love for Sale,* with trumpeter Ted Curson and tenor saxophonist Bill Barron. (One track from the latter session is issued here for the first time.) The Barnaby disk was recorded for the now

defunct Candid label. Originally recorded under bassist Buell
Neidlinger's name but never previously released, it has one
quartet track with Shepp and with Neidlinger and drummer
Dennis Charles as the rhythm section, two trio tracks with
Taylor, Neidlinger, and drummer Billy Higgins, and a remarkable medium-sized band version of Mercer Ellington's "Things
Ain't What They Used To Be," with Taylor, Shepp, Neidlinger,
Higgins, Steve Lacy, baritone saxophonist Charles Davis, trombonist Roswell Rudd, and, of all people, modern/mainstream
trumpeter Clark Terry. The Fantasy album was recorded live in
Copenhagen in 1962 with Jimmy Lyons and Sonny Murray. It
is the first recorded evidence of Taylor's new directions, in
which his music becomes at once sparer and more angular and
more complex, intense, and enigmatic. The second Blue Note
album is unique in that it features what is for Taylor a large
group (seven pieces) and introduces the highly individualistic
reed tones of Ken McIntyre to the Taylor/Lyons/Cyrille axis.
The Unit Core album (this is Taylor's own label), from 1973,
is Taylor, Lyons, and Cyrille playing two long tracks in which
Taylor's piano seems to have become even denser, his lines
more hotly melted into one another. The Arista/Freedom LP
is solo piano, recorded live at the Montreux Jazz Festival in
1974, and Taylor so fills every inch of space that it is suddenly
difficult to imagine him needing, or wanting, other musicians in
his band.

JOHN COLTRANE   *(1926–67)*

Coltrane's first instrument was E-
flat alto horn, which he started
playing in his high school band
in North Carolina, where he was
born and brought up. Later, he
switched to clarinet, and then,
apparently attracted by the music
of Johnny Hodges, to alto saxophone. After high school, he
joined his mother in Philadelphia, where she had gone to find
work, and attended the Ornstein
School of Music there.

His first jobs were with
rhythm-and-blues groups. The
most notable of these was with a
big band led by blues singer and alto saxophonist Eddie "Clean-
head" Vinson, whose requirements led Coltrane to play tenor
saxophone, the horn that eventually became his major instrument (although he also became one of the greatest soprano
saxophonists that jazz has ever known). In 1949, he went to
work for Dizzy Gillespie's big band, remaining with the trumpeter when the group was drastically pared down in size. In
1951, he returned to Philadelphia and took up music studies

again—this time, at the Granoff School of Music. Subsequently, he worked for bands led by jazz/rhythm-and-blues alto saxophonist Earl Bostic and by his old idol, Johnny Hodges.

In 1955, Coltrane was hired by Miles Davis, with whom he
was to remain—with some time out in 1957 to play with Thelonious Monk and to lead his own small bands—until 1960.
With Davis, Coltrane developed from a highly competent soloist into a true jazz star—especially in the second part of his association with the trumpeter. Like Sonny Rollins, whom he was
beginning to rival in popularity, Coltrane was an incomparably
solid, intelligent soloist who seemed to be able to combine all
the best elements of the bop and hard-bop idioms into his own
personal style. It was around 1959, in fact, that he first began
playing in the style that became his trade mark. Critic Ira Gitler
dubbed it "sheets of sound"—furiously fast juxtapositions of
chords that wove a seamless fabric of music.

Around the same time, Coltrane became interested in Eastern religions and Eastern music. His breakthrough album of
1959, the appropriately named *Giant Steps,* displayed Indian
modal concepts dramatically, and its freshness and conceptual
purity helped to establish him, once and for all, as a force to
be reckoned with in jazz. The next year, Coltrane made an album called *My Favorite Things,* which had a long, serpentine
soprano saxophone solo on the title track that has become an
undisputed jazz classic.

Also in 1960, Coltrane began an association with drummer
Elvin Jones and pianist McCoy Tyner, who were to form the
nucleus of his group until 1965, along with successive bassists
Steve Davis, Reggie Workman, and Jimmy Garrison. His albums of the mid-1960s with this group, which was sometimes
joined by Eric Dolphy, Pharoah Sanders, and/or another drummer, Rashied Ali, drift toward free jazz but still maintain ves-
tiges of conventional post-bop structure. In 1965, however,
Coltrane recorded a completely "free" record, *Ascension,* with
trumpeter Freddie Hubbard and saxophonists Archie Shepp
and John Tchicai. The same year, he also recorded an LP
called *A Love Supreme.* Its title track, based on an exceedingly
simple four-note motif and building from that into a searingly
hypnotic cry-filled solo by Coltrane, became a kind of anthem
of "new thing" spirituality and made the saxophonist something of a star to rock, as well as jazz audiences.

In 1965, there was a considerable acceleration in Coltrane's
previously gradual, zigzag journey to the outskirts of contemporary jazz. The modal aspects of his work faded, and his
sound became harsher, freer, more personal. Tyner and Jones
felt out of place with what he was doing and left the group;
shortly thereafter, so did Garrison. Coltrane's wife Alice joined
him on keyboards, harp, and vibraharp. Charlie Hadon played
bass with him on some sessions. Rashied Ali's part was augmented by other percussionists as Coltrane's music became
more heavily grounded in percussion. It also became more self-
consciously religious music; it is said that, shortly before his
death, Coltrane became a great admirer of Albert Einstein.

Coltrane had had health problems for much of his life, including a long and debilitating bout with heroin addiction in the 1950s. In addition, he was a compulsive eater, and so was often grossly overweight. In 1967, he began complaining of stomach trouble, but he seemed to have little faith in doctors. In the summer of that year, while in the hospital, he died of a liver ailment and various complications.

Both in his extraordinary post-bop playing of the late 1950s and in his later brilliant opening up of music in the 1960s, Coltrane seemed obsessively honest. He took in everything he heard, but he didn't steal it. He used the many resources available to him—his talent, his study of Western and Eastern musical theories, and his regular exposure to a succession of fine saxophonists from Eddie Vinson to Dolphy and Shepp—to forge a highly personal, carefully conceived style of playing. He jumped on no bandwagons, staying with traditional jazz values until he had good reason to believe that he had something sensible to replace them with.

Coltrane was not a founder of the avant-garde in jazz, but he became one of its most persuasive spokesmen. He is also probably its most influential single figure, because he has left his mark on far more individual musicians than Coleman, Taylor, Cherry, and Shepp—even if at least the first two were more responsible for dramatic changes in the music itself. Coltrane was, above all, a jazz personality. He was totally different from anyone else, and this drew other musicians to him, giving them sense of direction.

Selected Recordings:

More Lasting Than Bronze (two-record set, Prestige)
Giant Steps (Atlantic)
The Avant-Garde (Atlantic) by Coltrane and Don Cherry
My Favorite Things (Atlantic)
Live at the Village Vanguard (Impulse)
A Love Supreme (Impulse)
Ascension (Impulse)

The Prestige album is a two-record reissue of two good Coltrane LPs from 1957 and 1958, featuring the saxophonist in a rare trio context and with a quartet, quintet, and sextet. These include such musicians as trumpeter Donald Byrd, pianists Mal Waldron and Red Garland, and bassist Paul Chambers (the latter two also being Coltrane's colleagues in the Miles Davis unit of the time). Even at this rather early date, his playing is strong, confident, and not much like anybody else's. The first Atlantic disk is a classic, containing such well-known Coltrane compositions as the title tune, "Naima," "Cousin Mary," and "Syeeda's Song Flute," and hinting for the first time at the saxophonist's interest in modal song structures and solo plans. The second Atlantic album (which was actually recorded in 1960 but not released until six years later) includes three compositions by Ornette Coleman—the only important figure of the jazz avant-garde with whom Coltrane never recorded—and one each by Don Cherry (who shares co-credit as leader of the record) and Thelonious Monk. Cherry comes "in" a bit, rather than drawing Coltrane "out," but the latter's playing achieves a remarkable emotional intensity that rivals what Coleman was doing at the time. This LP also includes Coltrane's first recordings on soprano saxophone, although, because of the long delay in releasing it other recordings of him on this instrument were already available. The third Atlantic album was Coltrane's first really popular one, and his first whole record with Tyner and Jones. The Village Vanguard recording, which has Eric Dolphy on one track (on bass clarinet), shows vividly the richness and sincerity of feeling that Coltrane could convey.

A Love Supreme is important for the fiery extasis of the title track and for the compelling mixture of passion and calm the saxophonist seems able to convey throughout. The final two albums are mostly "free" Coltrane—the first featuring Freddie Hubbard, Archie Shepp, and John Tchicai, and the second featuring Pharoah Sanders. Both include a measure of what critics of free jazz call "honking and bleating," whereby each horn player retains a high degree of identifiable musical personality, with the leader himself cutting nicely through whatever else is going on, by dint of his speed, remarkable continuity of sound, and what might ultimately be called sheer character.

THE ART ENSEMBLE OF CHICAGO

In 1968, in Chicago, four musicians associated with pianist Muhal Richard Abrams's Association for the Advancement of Creative Music formed a highly ambitious, theatrical, and exhilarating original group dedicated (apparently) to the preservation, expression, and interfusion of all manner of jazz and other American, European, African, and Asian musical traditions. The result was the Art Ensemble of Chicago—an aggregation that has proved to be unclassifiable, astonishingly knowledgeable, admirably proficient, and usually great fun to listen to.

Founders of the group were saxophonists Joseph Jarman and Roscoe Mitchell (the group was originally called the Roscoe Mitchell Art Ensemble), trumpeter Lester Bowie, and bassist Malachi Favors. This remained the ensemble's personnel for several years—although drummer Don Moye has since joined the group. Bowie's wife, Fontella Bass, a singer who had some success as a rhythm-and-blues performer in the early 1960s, has worked with them as a guest artist. It must be stressed that the identifications of the musicians with their instruments describe primary affiliations only. A typical album jacket will credit each of them with an extraordinary variety of instruments.

Lester Bowie (1941–) was born in Maryland and brought up in Arkansas and Missouri. As a teenager, he played in rhythm-and-blues bands in the area, finally gravitating to Chicago, where he worked increasingly with jazz groups. He became associated with Muhal Richard Abrams, who was something of a guru (in the honest sense of the word) to young musicians in the city, and through him met the musicians who were to form the Art Ensemble with him. Bowie has recorded and performed widely with many important avant-garde players, including Archie Shepp, Alan Silva, Sonny Murray, Jimmy Lyons, and John Abercrombie. He is one of the most consistently exciting of the younger trumpeters in jazz today: it seems sometimes that he can make his horn say almost anything.

Roscoe Mitchell (1940–) was born and raised in Chicago and played saxophones in his high school band. He was a member of Abrams's big band, and then formed his own sextet, before co-founding the Art Ensemble. Like Bowie, he has worked with many figures in the jazz avant-garde, although he is less well-known as a soloist outside the AACM orbit than Bowie is.

Joseph Jarman (1937–) was born in Arkansas and brought up in Chicago. He studied music formally at the Chicago Conservatory of Music and wrote several avant-garde classical works before joining Abrams and company. He has worked less with other jazz players than Bowie and Mitchell have but has recorded several strong albums under his own name.

Malachi Favors (1937–) was born and raised in Chicago. He worked with pianist Andrew Hill for several years in the late 1950s, then joined Abrams's big band with Roscoe Mitchell. He recorded widely with members of the French and American avant-garde in France after joining the Art Ensemble, but has more recently played with that group most of the time.

Don Moye (1946–) was born in Rochester, New York, and grew up in Detroit, where he became involved with the local jazz avant-garde as a teenager. He traveled to Europe in 1968 with a group of Detroit musicians and stayed on for several years, playing with Steve Lacy, Gato Barbieri, Dave Burrell, and others. He met the other members of the Art Ensemble in Paris and returned to the United States with them as part of the group.

The Art Ensemble moved to Paris shortly after their formation, and when they elected to move back to the United States in 1971, it was because, Bowie said, "We miss the stimulation of the ghetto." Despite this, they have continued to travel frequently, and have remained particularly popular in France.

It is difficult to describe an Art Ensemble of Chicago performance. Moods change frequently; bitter anger, urbane flippancy, and great dancing charm trade fours. The breadth of musical styles involved is ultimately encyclopedic. There may be howling passages of free improvisation, dense thickets of African percussion, moments of sinuous Oriental delicacy, Basie-like riffs, references to Basin Street–type Dixieland, no-nonsense passages of hard bop, or any other music that fits. Just as it depends on jazz roots from the past, it is also a sterling example of how the avant-garde in jazz can enrich and renew all that has come before it.

Selected Recordings

A Jackson in Your House (BYG/Actuel)
Message to Our Folks (BYG/Actuel)
Les Stances à Sophie (Nessa)
Nice Guys (ECM)

The first LP on the French-based BYG/Actuel label (one that became known in the late 1960s for its recordings of fine French and American avant-garde jazz) has passages reminiscent of Southeast Asian music and of John Cage, and also contains quite a bit of spoken (militant) poetry. The second of them has an intricate satire of a gospel music call-and-response session, a reasonably straightforward (though certainly also forward-looking) version of Charlie Parker's classic "Dexterity," and a lengthy set piece, called "A Brain for the Seine," involving voice, lots of percussion, and plenty of "free" blowing. The Nessa disk, originally released in France on the EMI/Pathé label, is a soundtrack written and performed by the Art Ensemble and Fontella Bass for a film by Israeli/French director Moshe Mizrahi. It is the most accessible of the Art Ensemble's records and demonstrates articulately how skilled the Ensemble members are at hard, fast playing in what is, for them, a rather conventional idiom. The ECM LP, includes a hilarious reggae take-off called "Ja," and some tough, attractively dissonant hard bop.

–10–

Fusion and Beyond

Jazz, itself a fortuitous fusion (in both the correct and the common but incorrect sense of that adjective) of many musical styles and traditions, has never much seen the point of obsessive purity. Many of the elements that went into the making of jazz were also used, in various guises, in the popular and serious music of the early years of this century, and as soon as jazz was recognizable as a thing in itself, it, in turn, was borrowed, stolen, made fun of, and referred to in almost every other kind of music. Therefore, the practitioners of jazz seem to have felt completely justified in taking anything that they wanted from other kinds of music in return.

In the 1960s, the term "jazz/rock fusion," or simply "fusion," came to be applied to a kind of music that meshed elements of avant-garde and otherwise advanced jazz with elements of rhythm-and-blues and rock music—notably, the "heavy metal" variety, which is defined by its blistering guitar textures, its assertive and repetitive rhythms, and its high-volume use of electronic amplification and modulation.

The Beginnings
Just who the founders of jazz/rock fusion (hereafter referred to simply as fusion) were is hard to say. Fusion as we know it today grew out of two phenomena of the mid-to-late-1960s, both of which were related to the sudden, dramatic rise of rock music (as opposed to rock-and-roll, which is only one part of rock). Rock music was heralded by groups (mostly British, at first) like the Beatles and the Rolling Stones. On one hand, some of the better young rock musicians, most of whom were at least reasonably conversant with jazz, began looking for ways to bring it into their playing; on the other hand, jazz players, especially the younger ones, made efforts to become more "commercial" by accommodating some of the current rock vocabulary into their own work.

A group that has as good a claim as any to having been the first fusion band is the Free Spirits. This band, founded in 1966 by guitarist Larry Coryell and also featuring saxophonist Jim Pepper, played a rather self-conscious brand of music, into which Coryell's mostly ingenuous lyrics didn't fit very happily. It never appealed greatly to either devotees of jazz or to rock fans, and so it dissolved in short order. More durable early fusion groups included Jeremy and the Satyrs, led by flautist Jeremy Steig, and an English group called Soft Machine, formed by drummer Robert Wyatt, guitarist Daevid (sic) Allen, and keyboard player Mike Ratledge.

The first fusion group to achieve real popular success was not an electronic one. This band, Blood, Sweat & Tears, was formed in 1968. It brought rock its first jazz-oriented horn section and, for several years at least, one of its best Ray Charles-derived vocalists, David Clayton-Thomas. BS&T inspired numerous other groups, mostly (like them) ensembles of nine pieces or so that had strong horn sections. These included Chase, Tower of Power, and Chicago (originally the Chicago

Transit Authority)—the latter of which has proven to be even more durable than BS&T.

Horns, Guitars, and Keyboards

Despite BS&T, Chicago, and such, however, fusion has never been primarily a horn music. There are certainly individuals who are exceptions, among them trumpeter Donald Byrd, who forsook his solid bop origins to form a jazzy rhythm-and-blues group called the Blackbyrds, and Mike and Randy Brecker (saxophones and trumpet, respectively), who might be called the Dorsey Brothers of jazz/rock, having become greatly in demand as session musicians. More notably, there is saxophonist Wayne Shorter, another co-founder of Weather Report, and, of course, Miles Davis, who took from and gave to fusion exactly as much as he wanted to. In general, however the creators of fusion have been guitarists, keyboard players, bassists, and drummers—musicians playing those instruments that are most commonly found in rock.

Perhaps the most significant of these non-horn players is English guitarist John McLaughlin, who has played with many of the better jazz and rock musicians of the last fifteen years or so. His group, the Mahavishnu Orchestra, formed in 1971, defined many of the musical trademarks of fusion—electronic blurring of one instrument into another, drone-like bass patterns with the flavor of Indian classical music, long ascending and descending runs by guitar or keyboard matched, beat for beat, by drums, and other characteristic devices that have since become clichés.

Chick Corea

Two keyboard players have also been particularly important to fusion: Chick Corea and Herbie Hancock. Both have long and many-faceted careers in jazz. Corea worked with Latin-flavored jazz bands led by Mongo Santamaria, Willie Bobo, and Herbie Mann in the early 1960s. In 1968, he recorded his own debut album as a leader, and, later in the year, he joined Miles Davis, with whom he played off and on for several years. In 1970, Corea bassist Dave Holland, and drummer Barry Altschul formed a trio that had leanings toward the avant-garde. This group, which became known as Circle, leaned still farther out with the addition of reed player Anthony Braxton in 1971. Late that year, Corea disbanded Circle and went to work briefly with bop saxophonist Stan Getz. In 1972, he changed direction again, forming Return to Forever with reed player Joe Farrell, bassist Stanley Clarke, and the Brazilian husband-and-wife team of percussionist Airto Moreira (here playing regular jazz drums) and vocalist Flora Purim. Return to Forever was originally a light-textured, Brazilian-flavored, partially electronic jazz group, but gradually, the personnel and character of the group changed. A succession of guitarists replaced Farrell, and vocals were downplayed. The volume and the use of electronics went up, and soon the group had become an out-and-out fusion band—one of the best, most intensely exciting, most popular of them. At least three one-time members of Return to Forever have gone on to become fusion stars in their own right: drummer Lenny White, guitarist Al DiMeola, and bassist Stanley Clarke. Corea himself has continued to work with Farrell, Moreira, Purim, and other former colleagues in contexts outside Return to Forever, and regularly releases albums under his own name that blend not only jazz and rock or rhythm-and-blues, but also various musical elements, including Spanish and Latin American music, into intense programmatic pieces that are difficult to classify. He has also recently toured and recorded with fellow pianist Herbie Hancock—with both men playing "old-fashioned" acoustic pianos.

Herbie Hancock

Herbie Hancock, born in Chicago in 1940, had his own successful hard bop group in the early 1960s (for which he wrote and recorded "Watermelon Man", which later became a sizable hit for Mongo Santamaría). He played with Miles Davis from 1963 to 1968, then formed a superb sextet with reed player Bennie Maupin, trombonist Julian Priester, trumpeter Eddie Henderson, bassist Buster Williams, and drummer Billy Hart that lasted for three years or so. Hancock began utilizing electric and electronic instruments with the group, even adding synthesizer player Pat Gleeson to the personnel at one point; but although it was one of the best, most intelligently forward-looking small bands in jazz, it never really was a fusion band. In 1973, Hancock formed a group, the Headhunters, that was firmly in the fusion camp. It retained Maupin, replaced the other two horn players with guitarists, and went unabashedly electronic (although Hancock himself has also kept his ties with other kinds of music). The Headhunters, with and without Hancock, has continued to be one of the most commercially successful of all fusion bands, if not *the* most. It was also the first important electronic fusion group (as opposed to the horn-oriented BS&T type) to turn its back almost entirely on the jazz avant-garde and work into a funky, almost purely rhythm-and-blues idiom.

It is hard to know how to classify trumpeter Chuck Mangione. He is not a fusion player in the usual sense, but his works with large orchestra and his own smaller groups have indeed been fusions of a kind, incorporating jazz, rock, pop, and classical orchestral elements into a kind of lush, jazz-like music that is easy to listen to and usually characterized by beautiful, simple, melodic lines.

Jazz and Fusion

It is often difficult today to know where fusion stops and the rest of jazz begins. A great number of jazz players of all disciplines have recorded at least occasionally with some of the trappings of fusion (and even, more recently, of disco)—among them, such well-established figures as Count Basie, Woody Herman, Maynard Ferguson, Buddy Rich, Dizzy Gillespie, Sonny Rollins, Horace Silver, Cedar Walton, Freddie Hubbard, Hubert Laws, Jean-Luc Ponty, and Bobby Hutcherson. It is not an insult to their memories to say that if Charlie Parker and John Coltrane were still alive, they would certainly have recorded by now over throbbing rhythm-and-blues-style bass lines and waves of electric keyboard sounds. They would probably even use amplified, electronically modulated saxophones.

Diehard jazz fans object to fusion (and music that is close to fusion) on the grounds that it substitutes volume and technological trickery for musical imagination—a valid objection in some cases. They also maintain that fusion tends to obscure artistic individuality, frequently blending instruments electronically so that they seem to have no separate dynamic or tonal values of their own. This is sometimes so extreme that it is almost impossible to differentiate between the various keyboard and stringed instruments, and sometimes even the horns.

The obvious answer to the argument, although it is not without merit, is that jazz has never been immune to what has been going on around it musically—and shouldn't be: every stylistic turnaround in jazz has been decried by supporters of an earlier aesthetic, but every one has finally been accepted into the fold. It is also in fusion's favor that it has brought fine jazz musicians into the spotlight, earning them a measure of commercial success and identification by younger audiences that jazz has too long been denied.

Beyond Fusion

What lies beyond fusion? It is too soon to tell for sure, but it seems likely that at least part of the answer is that we will be hearing the same things that came before fusion. No new movement in jazz has ever completely destroyed earlier jazz styles, and it seems safe to predict that no new movement ever will. There are traditional jazz "preservation" or "revival" societies all over the world, playing music not unlike that heard in New Orleans in the first two decades of this century. Reincarnations of swing-era big bands play at dance concerts all over the United States, and some of the most famous musicians of that period—Roy Eldridge, Count Basie, Benny Carter, Benny Goodman—are still alive and swinging. Younger musicians, too, are studying and ultimately embracing older styles. Mike Lipskin became a protégé of the great stride pianist Willie "The Lion" Smith. Brooks Kerr, another of Smith's followers, became such an expert on Ellingtonia that when he was not yet 25, Ellington said of him that he knew more Ellington compositions than Ellington himself. Others are Eldridge-influenced cornetist Warren Vaché, and tenor saxophonist Scott Hamilton, whose muse is Ben Webster.

Bop, too, is still feverishly alive. A kind of modern mainstream has grown up that is not afraid of electronic and/or other rock influences, that often utilizes Eastern or South American elements, but is grounded firmly in bop and even blues. Much of this particular brand of jazz appears on the German-based ECM label, which regularly brings together top European, American, and sometimes Japanese and South American jazz players to record music that often ranges, even on a single cut, from the elegantly "free" to the soporifically beautiful. The undisputed star of the label, and one of the most commercially successful of the younger jazz players in any idiom, is pianist Keith Jarrett, whose accessible, eclectic style and obsession with technical perfection make him perhaps the definitive jazz musician of the early 1980s.

WEATHER REPORT

As a young man Austrian-born keyboard player Joe Zawinul (1932–   ) became popular as a session pianist in his native country, playing with many of the top local bands, including one led by composer/pianist Fredrich Gulda. In 1959, he emigrated to America, where he found work with the Maynard Ferguson band and trombonist Slide Hampton's group and became Dinah Washington's accompanist for a year and a half. In 1961, he joined the Cannonball Adderly group. He remained with them for nearly a decade, writing numerous compositions for them (including the Grammy-winning "Mercy, Mercy, Mercy") and arranging several albums for both Cannonball and Nat Adderly. He also pursued an independent career as a sideman, working with musicians like Coleman Hawkins, Ben Webster, and Oliver Nelson, and ultimately made several albums under his own name, including *The Rise and Fall of the Third Stream*. He also appeared on four key Miles Davis albums, including *In a Silent Way* (for which he wrote the title track) and *Bitches' Brew*.

The career of saxophonist Wayne Shorter (1933–   ) has had some surprising parallels with Zawinul's. The Newark-born musician started freelancing around New York, playing tenor saxophone, at about the time that Zawinul arrived in the United States, and like Zawinul, he played for a time with Maynard Ferguson. In 1959, he joined Art Blakey's Jazz Messengers, a band whose blues-influenced hard bop wasn't terribly different from Adderly's. In 1964, Shorter went to work for Miles Davis, with whom he remained until 1970 and with whom he began to play soprano as well as tenor saxophone.

In 1971, Zawinul and Shorter joined forces to create a jazz group that would be, as much as possible, free from labels or stylistic restrictions. They wanted to be able to put their considerable, and sometimes similar, experience together with their ideas about the directions that jazz might take. In Zawinul's case, this included highly imaginative utilization of electronics and a tendency toward what has been called "space music"— in the extraterrestial sense of the term; however, both he and Shorter wanted to produce a brand of music that was part fusion, part avant-garde, part modern mainstream, but also, in large part, something of their own. They named the group Weather Report.

Besides Zawinul and Shorter, the original personnel of the group included bassist Miroslav Vitous, drummer Alphonse Mouzon, and percussionist Airto Moreira. According to some reports at the time of the band's first album, Vitous was an equal co-founder of Weather Report with Zawinul and Shorter, but Zawinul has subsequently said that this is not true.

There have been numerous personnel changes, but, in any case, Zawinul and Shorter clearly are Weather Report: whoever their colleagues have been, they have continuously produced a complex, stylistically varied, well-played music that is very much their own and decidedly worth hearing.

Selected Recordings

The Rise and Fall of the Third Stream by Joe Zawinul (Vortex)
Mountain in the Clouds by Miroslav Vitous (Atlantic)
Odyssey of Iska by Wayne Shorter (Blue Note)
Native Dancer by Wayne Shorter (Columbia)
I Sing the Body Electric (Columbia)
Talespinnin' (Columbia)
Black Market (Columbia)

The Zawinul album is a fine example of an earlier kind of "fusion" music, the jazz/classical Third Stream period. The leader's hard-driving piano (and, occasionally, electric piano) is fitted neatly into William Fischer's string arrangements, and the jazz feeling is strong and authentic throughout. The Vitous recording, from 1969, is rather more straightforward: the band includes Joe Henderson, John McLaughlin, Herbie Hancock, and Jack DeJohnette or Joe Chambers. The Shorter Blue Note album presents the saxophonist as the sole horn against an unusual group composed of vibraharp (or marimba), guitar, two basses (Ron Carter and Cecil McBee, who are about as good as musicians come), and three drummers/percussionists. There is a haunting, lyrical quality to the music that anticipates some of Shorter's quieter moments with Weather Report. Even more lyrical is the Shorter LP on Columbia, which features Brazilian guitarist/vocalist Milton Nascimento and five of his songs. The first Weather Report album—in fact, the group's second recording—with Vitous, Gravatt, and Romao, contains a particularly haunting track called "The Moors" and some electrifying live material recorded in Japan. The second disk, with Johnson, Ndugu, and Lima, is mostly Zawinul's album, with his arsenal of instruments (including electric and acoustic pianos, various synthesizers, Melodica, organ, xylophone,· and miscellaneous percussion) weaving thick textures in which Shorter is a highlight, an accent. The third album, with Pastorius, Thompson, and Acuna (and Johnson, Alias, and Walden on some tracks), has a particularly festive mood about it and shows neatly how well Zawinul and Shorter have integrated their music, each into the other's.

JOHN MCLAUGHLIN *(1942–   )*

Born in Yorkshire, England, McLaughlin taught himself to play the guitar as a boy. In his late teens, he started working in blues and rock groups in London—most notably, those led by keyboard players Graham Bond and Brian Auger. He became associated with the British avant-garde rock and jazz scene, working with Jack Bruce and, briefly, with jazz and pop singer Georgie Fame. In 1968, English bassist Dave Holland recommended him to drummer Tony Williams, who had just left Miles Davis to form his own fusion band, Lifetime. McLaughlin emigrated to America to join Williams and was soon working with Davis as well, appearing on the pivotal albums *In a Silent Way* and *Bitches' Brew.*

McLaughlin made his debut as a leader (or, rather, a co-leader) on an album made in 1970 with saxophonist John Surman. Early in 1971, McLaughlin embraced the teachings of an Indian guru, Sri Chinmoy Kumar Ghose and, under his influence, added the name "Mahavishnu" to his own name. He recorded an innovative album with avant-garde bassist Charlie Haden, percussionist Airto Moreira, Indian percussionist Badal Roy, saxophonist Dave Liebman, drummer Billy Cobham, and violinist Jerry Goodman.

Shortly after recording that album, McLaughlin formed a regular group, which he called the Mahavishnu Orchestra. It included Cobham and Goodman, the Czech keyboard player Jan Hammer, and the Irish bassist Rick Laird. For the two years that it lasted, this quintet was probably the most exciting, proficient, influential electronic jazz group in the world. In 1973, however, the group disbanded so that its members could pursue their own careers. McLaughlin formed a larger version of the Mahavishnu group for a time and recorded with jazz-leaning rock guitarist Carlos Santana, who was also a disciple of Sri Chinmoy. In 1975, McLaughlin broke off with the guru and dropped "Mahavishnu" from his name.

He next worked with a band composed entirely of Indian musicians that shaped his music into Indian forms. That group broke up in 1978, but he retained the Indian violinist, L. Shankar, for his new group, the One Truth Band.

McLaughlin is one of the technical wonders of the contemporary guitar, not only for exceptional ability as a guitarist (unlike some of his contemporaries, he has continued to incorporate acoustic passages into his work), but for his great understanding of the powers and limitations of electronics. He retains elements of a straightforward jazz style but has successfully incorporated into his playing an extremely wide range of other influences, like Indian music, rock and blues, and even classical forms. All of these qualities are integrated into his basic style with great intelligence and apparent ease. He is a sensible virtuoso.

Selected Recordings

Extrapolations (Polydor)
My Goal's Beyond (Douglas)
The Inner Mounting Flame (Columbia)
Shakti with John McLaughlin (Columbia)
Electric Dreams (Columbia)

The Polydor LP, with John Surman, has little to suggest fusion about it, tending, as it does, towards free improvisation; but McLaughlin's style sounds already fully formed, and he is recognizable as the man who will later become the best of the fusion guitarists. The Douglas record is more complex and delicate and includes an especially warm-hearted version of Charles Mingus's tribute to Lester Young, "Goodbye Pork-Pie Hat." The first Columbia album is the Mahavishnu Orchestra's debut recording and shows well how cohesive and exhilarating a group they were. The second Columbia is the first Shakti album. It is distinctly Indian in flavor, with some extremely beautiful moments of interplay between McLaughlin and L. Shankar's violin. The final Columbia disk is the first recording by the One Truth Band. The Indian flavor is minimal, and there are moments of reasonably straight jazz that are reminiscent of McLaughlin's earlier work.

KEITH JARRETT   *(1945–   )*

Jarrett started taking piano lessons in his home town of Allentown, Pennsylvania, when he was extremely young. At the age of 7, he played his first concert, and he has performed regularly from that time on. He attended the Berklee School in Boston on a scholarship and formed his own jazz group in that city.

In 1965, he moved to New York and began freelancing. He played with Art Blakey's Jazz Messengers for several months, then joined a group led by flautist/tenor saxophonist Charles Lloyd that also included Jack DeJohnette. With Lloyd's group, Jarrett became something of a new star as a pianist. Lloyd featured him generously, nearly always including at least one unaccompanied Jarrett piano solo in his sets. Jarrett's style, alternately gospel-jazzy and energetically avant-garde (he frequently attacked the piano strings directly or pounded various parts of the piano to set the strings vibrating), won him fans all over the world—Lloyd's group being very popular overseas.

Jarrett made his own first recordings in 1968, with a trio including Charlie Haden and drummer Paul Motian. In the early 1970s, he joined Miles Davis for a time, then formed his own quartet with Haden, Motian, and saxophonist Dewey Redman. At about the same time, he made a beautiful solo piano album called *Facing You* for the ECM label. This record first gained him a following of impassioned fans that was almost a cult, an enthusiasm that later spread to the general public. The chief reason for his popularity is Jarrett's unusual, supremely engaging style of solo improvisation, in which he uses repeated bass figures, happily familiar blues and gospel chords, dramatic changes of key and tempo, dazzling runs, and references to a score of other piano styles from Tatum to Powell to Evans to Taylor (and Nashville pianist Floyd Cramer, Mal Waldron, and Ray Bryant) and back again—all adding up to his own hypnotic, technically beautiful kind of music.

More recently, Jarrett has worked with a quartet including Danish bassist Palle Danielsson, drummer Jon Christensen, and Norwegian saxophonist Jan Garbarek. He has also written and helped to perform large-scale orchestral and chamber works, has recorded a double album of improvisations on an 18th-century German pipe organ, and has occasionally recorded as a sideman with other musicians.

Jarrett takes his music (and, some critics say, himself) very seriously, imbuing it with mystical worth. All this has led some observers to denigrate Jarrett's playing and to consider him to be an overrated musician. Nevertheless, Jarrett has been, and, for the most part, remains a supremely gifted jazz player with a great knowledge of jazz and respect for its past. More often than not, his music provides a most compelling way of making jazz come alive.

Selected Recordings

Life Between the Exit Signs (Vortex)
Facing You (ECM)
Solo Concerts, Bremen/Lausanne (ECM)
In the Light (ECM)
The Köln Concert (ECM)
Hymns/Spheres (ECM)
Byablue (Impulse)
Tales of Another by Gary Peacock (ECM)
My Song (ECM)

The Vortex album is young Jarrett, circa 1968, with Haden and Motian. There are some of the pianist's characteristically symmetrical melodies here, as well as some of the non-traditional percussive use of the piano that first won him public notice. (The ghost of Henry Cowell was invariably summoned up by critics speaking of the early Jarrett.) The first ECM LP was Jarrett's impressive debut as a pianist playing solo for an entire album. It is elegantly crafted, much calmer than his later solo work, and, unlike it, is broken into a number of short compositions instead of a few lengthy improvisations.

The Bremen and Lausanne concerts, on solo piano, are presented in a three-record set and are a splendid representation of Jarrett's (solo) improvisational and technical repertoire. Listening to him at this length, one comes to appreciate the cautiousness with which he builds his solos and his gift for combining elements that are largely familiar (and even sometimes over-familiar) into interesting, attractive pieces of music. *In the Light* is a two-record set devoted to Jarrett's "serious" (that is, non-jazz or only vaguely jazz-like) compositions: a string quartet, a brass quintet, a "fughata" for harpsichord, a piece for four cellos and two trombones, a "Short Piece for Guitar and Strings," a piece for piano, gong, percussion, and strings, a work for flute and strings, and a solo piano piece. Jarrett plays piano (even on the work for harpsichord), gong, and percussion and conducts two of the works. The compositions are quite pleasant, rather ordinary music in the early-20th-century French style. The string quartet works particularly well, and the solo piano passages are not unlike Jarrett's jazz piano records, except that they employ slightly more dissonance. The Köln recording, also a two-record set, is perhaps Jarrett's best-known solo work: it is quite similar to the Bremen/Laussanne album, but the themes are even more engaging, and several of the lines are particularly hypnotic. *Hymns/Spheres* is an ambitious album of solo organ pieces played on the "Trinity Organ" built by Karl Joseph Riepp for the Benedictine Abbey om Ottobeuren (in what is now West Germany) in the mid-18th century. The themes are stately and rather somber, recalling Messiaen and Duruflé far more than Jimmy Smith or Jack McDuff. The Impulse recording is a strong example of Jarrett's Redman/Haden/Motian quartet. The title theme, played in two versions—by the quartet and in piano solo—is especially attractive, and Redman's tenor saxophone is a delight throughout. Jarrett also plays some soprano saxophone here. The Gary Peacock LP, with Jarrett on piano, Peacock on bass, and Jack DeJohnette on drums, is wonderful, straight-ahead jazz that demonstrates what a fine bassist Peacock really is and how well he can spur on a pianist. Jarrett is at his most imaginative and energetic, even though he is playing somebody else's music and performing in an unaccustomed context. The last album is by Jarrett and the Scandinavians who completed his quartet at this time: Garbarek, Danielsson, and Christensen. Garbarek is a rather cold, though technically proficient saxophonist (he plays both soprano and tenor saxophones here, although the latter is his regular instrument), and the album lacks the emotional intensity that Jarrett's work with the Redman quartet has; but the pianist is in good form, and there are some long, lovely thematic lines performed.